Hello
my name is

BIPOLAR

Justin Bailey

HELLO MY NAME IS BIPOLAR

Justin Bailey

PREFACE

My name is Justin Bailey, and for the past 15 years Mental Illness
has been a part of my everyday life. From the moment I wake up
in the morning, to my dreams at night, It impacts every second of
everyday.

Some of us are able to find a means of therapy right away, and have
the tools and resources to cope and overcome. Most of us do not.

Mental Illness impacts everyone in one way, shape, or form.
Impacting not just us, but also the people in our lives that we care
about the most. As life's pressure and stresses continue to mount,
Mental Illness impacts more and more people every day.

For many men like myself, Mental Illness is a 'stigma' or sign of
weakness that is just so hard to admit. For as strong as the male
in society is 'supposed to be', it can be downright debilitative
stopping us dead in our tracks. For most of us the biggest
challenge is admitting that we have a problem, and asking for help
to fix it.

I am not a Doctor, a Licensed Clinician, nor a Therapist. I am in
no position to provide medical advice. However my story comes
directly from the perspective of the inflicted. What it's like getting
into the head of the one experiencing it on a daily basis.

Whether it was getting shot at a mass shooting, the shit-show
that was my rehab, crazy stories of rideshare driving and my
lawsuit and win therein…I've put myself through a lot – probably
more than I should have.

My purpose for sharing my story is to help anyone that can relate understand that there is a way out. If I can help people from experiencing the pain that I had gone through, or help shorten the duration therein – then my purpose has been fulfilled. Thank you for reading my story.

Sincerely,
Justin

CHAPTER I. EVERYONE HAS A PLAN UNTIL THEY GET SHOT

It is difficult for me to recount something that I've worked so hard to put behind me. However, this is the night that changed my life forever, there is no way I'll ever forget. I was 24 years old, a few years out of college, with the career I'd always dreamed of. As a young professional I still had a lot of friends with super senior status, still enjoying the regularity of weekend college parties, and this was my night to indulge as well. At the time I had a very close-knit group of friends I had done almost everything with since my freshman year at Sacramento State University.

The weekend before we had attended the Zone Ball, a huge Halloween Costume Party at Cal Expo where they hold the annual state fair in the summer. We were among the hundreds of partygoers adorning the most creative of costumes. My friends and I leading up to this event wanted to show up decked out in a themed group of costumes – this year we were Mario Kart racers. We had Mario, Luigi, Toad, Donkey Kong, and I was Bowser. One of my best friends had worked at Costco and brought everyone these oversized fruit boxes – you know the type you put your 4-dozen eggs and 5-lbs of butter in to transport to your car. We put a lot of effort into painting and fashioning these boxes to look like Mario Karts. We had made suspenders to hang the karts off of our shoulders, and pretty sure some of ours came equipped with the ever-so-important cupholders. I dressed as Bowser, the villain of the game, had a bright red wig and made a spiked turtle shell that I sewed together with pieces of felt and a pillow as filling. The comradery and closeness we had as friends personified by our group costume, we had a blast and everyone had a blast with us. We just wanted to have fun, get kinda fucked up, and see what kind of memories we could make. In hindsight, we all would've been so much better off if we had left the party there that night, but we all agreed to an encore the next weekend at Patrick's house next door.

October 31st 2008 was a Friday, the party was going to be so epic we'd have two nights to sleep off the hangover. I had finished a half-day at the office. The company I worked for had a lot of young families, and always did a great job decorating for the holidays to make it an experience our coworkers could bring there children in to enjoy – and Halloween was always the most fun. So I had a pretty chill day eating pot luck and handing out candy to the dozens of kids that would snake through our cubicles adorning the cutest of costumes.

That evening my girlfriend at the time, who would be my future wife, had plans to visit a co-worker's house party before we met up with our other friends at Patrick's house to finish up the night.

Tim's party was way out off West Sunrise Blvd. It was a little out of the way for us but I couldn't miss seeing my half-plastered coworkers dressed up playing games. I remember Tim's costume still vividly to this day – he was dressed up in a robe as the Dude from Big Lebowski. That's still one of my favorite movies and for a while there my drink of choice to bring to gatherings often included vodka, Kahlua, and cream - the movie's signature drink The White Russian.

Hindsight is a word that I have difficulty with. People will say in hindsight, I may have done this differently, knowing now what I didn't know then. Fuck hindsight, yeah no shit If I would have known now what I didn't then – yeah my life would be different.

Tim didn't want us to leave, he wanted us to finish out the evening with them, almost in a cryptic way thinking back as we had no idea what was instore ahead. We left Tim's party and headed west on hwy 50 to an area near Sacramento State off Watt Avenue and La Riviera Drive called College Greens where a lot of college kids lived. My best friends had rented a house 1 door down from a park where we'd play sloshball – a kind of baseball game that involved a keg at second base where the winner wasn't the team with the most runs because by the end of the game we were so hammered there was no way we could keep score. Their next door neighbor was a house rented by Patrick and a few of his friends. He had a gorgeous girlfriend, and a red dog named Jager everyone adored. Wherever Patrick was, Jager was always at his side. We would go over to Patrick's place to have parties and play beer pong. He also used to order the UFC fights where we'd all kick down to drink, eat pizza, and watch the fights together. After some time went by, some of my friends had graduated and moved out of the house next door to Patrick's, but we still found ourselves there often to meet up.

We had gotten to the party a little later in the evening, so the street they lived on was already packed with cars. We parked down the street, and my girlfriend and I agreed that if for whatever reason we were to get separated - we would always meet up at the car.

So we walk in, and the place was packed. As we made our way through the crowded living room and into the kitchen that connected to the backyard. I'd see my group of friends, all decked out in their Mario Kart costumes as was I, we gave our customary bro hugs and quickly got started on getting after it. Now like many parties that we went to whether in college or after, there were always people we didn't know, but they were always friends of friends that belonged.

I hung out with a group of people that were accepting of those from all ethnicities, cultures, and backgrounds. As long as everyone had fun, were respectful of the house, and played well with others there was no issue. However it was common when parties got too out of hand and people were there that shouldn't be, and people would start fighting.

That was the worst case scenario, there's an argument over a girl or someone drank from someone else's bottle and a few punches would be thrown but it never really escalated into much more than that. As hosts or friends of the host, if people got out of hand, we knew that we had numbers and that if something happened we would jump in to make things right. That night there were so many of us friends, and after sizing anyone up that looked like they may be there to start problems - I felt confident that if something happened I could hold my own.

There was a turning point in that night where things were a little off. A group of 7 guys had shown up, that would not have necessarily looked out of place, if it weren't for the demeanor for which they were acting. For lack of a better term these guys were 'thugged out.'

It wasn't the fact they were black - we had friends there that were black. It wasn't because they had dreadlocks and bloodshot eyes – we had friends with dreadlocks and I sure as shit had some pretty bloodshot eyes that night too. But these guys were kinda 'mean-mugging' the whole time. I remember meeting one of them in the kitchen and offered to make them a drink, as offering a drink was something of a welcoming act that would maybe in hopes defuse any tension they were exuding. He asked me If I wanted to buy some 'thizz' slang for ecstasy, which I didn't have any interest in doing. We were drinking and there were definitely blunts in abundance being passed around – and that was really as far as my party ever got.

Things for me progressed and I was pretty fucked up at that point. The party was basically broken out in 3 areas, the living room and kitchen, the backyard, and the garage. The garage was decked out in beer pong tables, and there were probably 4 games going all at once throughout the night. My girlfriend was with my friends in the garage playing beer pong, and so I knew she was safe.

I'm in the backyard with some other friends, and I notice my friend and party-host Patrick pacing the backyard. He was saying that one of his friends' cameras was missing, and it was the group of 7 that I had initial concerns with, that he was accusing of stealing her camera.

At this moment the only thing I can remember is that I had to pee really bad, and it was customary for gentlemen at parties to allow the restroom for females (as there was always a line to get in) and for us 'gentlemen' to find a spot outside. So I was peeing on the back fence. I remember I really had to pee, so it was an instant relief. It was such a long pee, it felt like it would last an eternity. The story from there I still remember so vividly happened so fast. So fast I didn't have a chance to finish peeing on the back fence to realize what was happening.

Out of the corner of my right eye I could see Patrick was incredibly agitated talking to his friends about the stolen camera, and how it had been these guys. He was so insulted that someone he would graciously allow to party with us would come with such nefarious purposes. He was hopping around, I could tell at this moment he was getting himself hyped up to go fight these guys. I remember a few friends of his trying to hold him back and calm him down - - all while I see the group of 7 just a few feet away. I later would find out they were putting their hoodies on, as an attempt to not be identified for what they were about to do.

It all happened just so fast, I don't think I was able to finish peeing when I saw Patrick rush this group that I could only describe as two masses of people smashing into each other. It was like both of these groups were shot out of a cannon right at each other. Mind you the worst we could imagine of this was a big fistfight. But the group of 7 had no intentions on throwing fists. I can't remember if I saw the muzzle flashes, or heard the shots first, but they almost felt like two different separate sensations. I don't recall exactly how many shots were actually fired, it seemed like he unloaded the full clip so maybe a dozen or so. As soon as the gun shots went off, the party turned into a frenzy, where people in the back yard were hopping the fence into the adjacent park until someone kicked down an entire section of the fence, and you had the mass exodus of people scurrying trying to find a place out of harm's way. I think it took me a few seconds to digest what was actually happening, to hear the shots and see the muzzle flashes, and interpret why everyone was fleeing the way they were.

Only then did I try to take a step and felt my entire lower left leg go numb. In mere seconds the entire backyard was cleared out, all that were left were those that were shot and a few friends who would turn out to be heroes to help us wounded. I could tell by the khaki Dickies I was wearing that I was shot in the calf. The bullet went through the back of my leg, bounced off my shin and shooting out the front of my leg ultimately breaking my Tibia. I had some brand new black Nike Shox shoes, and my left foot was soaked in warm blood. At that point I really didn't know what had happened, or how bad it had really gotten.

Matt was one of my best friends, and he was there to help me. He put my arm around him and he helped me over to the patio table and chairs. He took off his t-shirt and wrapped it around my leg and tied it as a tourniquet. He propped my leg up on the patio table and stayed there with me holding the tourniquet tight. I'm not sure how much blood one can lose from that type of trauma, I don't know if he hadn't helped would I have had the wherewithal to do it myself. I had been drinking so much, could have I bled out that night, maybe. But I had Matt there by my side to make sure I didn't.

There are images, more so the scenes that would play out from there that still haunt my dreams to this day. I cannot and I don't know If I'll ever be able to forget or come to peace with what happened next – but it sure fucked me up pretty good.

Again I didn't know how many people had gotten shot at that point. I thought and hoped that it was only me. Then I saw Patrick. Patrick was laying face up with his arms out, no more than 10 feet away from where I was seated at the patio. Patrick was shot once in the forehead. Patrick was lying in a pool of his own blood. Patrick's dog Jager right there with him, his nose nudging

Patrick's face in almost a manner to wake him up. The confusion on that dog's face, not knowing what had happened, but knowing his loyal and loving companion was no longer there is something I still struggle with mightily. This compounded with the wail of screams from his girlfriend. The "Why?", the "Please don't go", the "Oh my Gods" – that scene plays out in my head like it was just yesterday here 15 years later.

At this point I had learned that there were 3 others that were also shot. Two guys were shot in their arms respectively, and one was shot in the stomach. I learned this as First Responders and Paramedics canvassed the backyard, and deemed me the least injured of the group. It may have been a total of 20 minutes until I was taken out on a stretcher, but it felt like an eternity.

At this point the only thing that was on my mind was, is my girlfriend okay? I had to think positively, and knowing that she was in the garage, away from where the shooting occurred and with friends that would keep her safe, I could only hope that she was alright. Nothing would have been worse that night than to have to go to her parents with the news that something happened to her because of a place that I took her. She was everything to me at that point, and is still one of the most important people in my life. As I was brought out through the garage and out to the front yard where the ambulance was ready to take me away – I saw her, and I felt an immediate feeling of relief. The amount of time I was in that back yard was I guess enough time for her to call my brother and her parents, and they were there outside as I came out. My only way to diffuse tension and let everyone know I was okay, was to give a thumbs up with a smile. Emotionally I hadn't fully realized the gravity of what had happened that night until days later. It may have been that humor was always my go to. It may have been the adrenaline – as I didn't feel any pain for hours. It was all so surreal – but one thing was for certain Patrick was dead, and myself and 3 other survivors were left picking up the pieces as to what happened to us and where do we go from here?

CHAPTER II. THE AFTERMATH

I arrived at UC Davis Medical Center by ambulance where I was ushered into what looked like a triage staging area, with beds surrounding the perimeter of the room separated by curtains. I would later learn that Halloween is one of the most deadliest holidays. I was told that there were other shootings throughout Sacramento that night, so my group wasn't the only ones there and it was a little chaotic. I remember as the adrenaline started to wear off they had given me morphine for the pain – I remember distinctly the warming sensation it gave me. I wasn't in pain anymore, and with everything that had happened and the fact that I was pretty hammered upon my arrival, I couldn't yet make sense of what really had happened. I had been interviewed by detectives in the emergency room as my wounds were being treated. I remember them asking me if I had seen the shooter, or if I recognized any of those involved – and I really didn't have a clue. The only things I could remember were that they were all black, most if not all had dreadlocks, and they were small, skinny, and all looked pretty young.

They had set my leg back into place, bandaged me up, ordered prescriptions for me to pick up on my way home and I was sent on my way. My brother had alerted my parents – I'm sure receiving that phone call at 1:00 am was pretty frightening for them. I connected with them and they had come to visit me either that day or the next. By this time all of my friends had heard about what had happened, and I was receiving all kinds of texts like "Holy shit are you okay?" and "Fuck Man that shit is crazy." Within

24 hours I had to go to the sheriff's office for a formal interview. Candidly I wasn't a great witness, as I was under the influence, it was dark out, I had never seen these guys before and didn't spend much time focusing on them at all during the party. They showed me a photo lineup, and I accidentally laughed looking at one mugshot. "This guy's ugly as fuck, I'd sure remember his face if I saw it before." Humor was my defense mechanism in that state. I took it as seriously as one would knowing that it could lead to the shooter, and ultimately provide Patrick's family some justice.

After leaving the sheriff's office we went to a friend's house where everyone had gathered to talk about what had happened. At this point there were a lot of rumors flying around as to who did this. Was this a planned shooting? Some thought because it was Halloween night it could have been a gang initiation. Maybe we were targeted because we were so inviting, welcoming in complete strangers under the premise we were all there to have a good time. These were all fair theories, but at that time they were all just that – theories.

That day I had called my boss to tell him I wouldn't be going in to work the next Monday – my cushy white-collar desk job – because I had been shot at a party the night prior. I could only imagine what he was thinking when I told him what had happened. They were incredibly supportive, and gave me as much time as I needed before coming back. Within the office I had built quite the celebrity profile with this, as it was so far-fetched that anything like that would happen to one of them – and sure as shit I was living proof that it did. The outpouring of well-wishing at that time is one of the reasons why I still consider some of those former colleagues as best friends to this day. I guess when you go through trauma like that – you really take stock in what and who are most important to you, and upon my recovering I was welcomed back with open arms. I would be forever grateful.

About a week afterwards I had gone back to the hospital for a check-up, and would ultimately go through one of the most painful experiences ever. When assessing my injury they realized that the soft cast they put me in at the hospital wasn't sturdy enough. They were concerned I would have "drop foot," as my ankle was stuck at like a 70 degree angle. This created tightness in my Achilles tendon and unless they were able to push it back to a 45 degree angle, they would have to surgically repair my Achilles to create that range of motion I would need to walk again. Mind you I had just been shot a week prior and now they were forcing my leg into a walking boot and forcefully yanking my leg forward until it set in at their desired 45 degree angle – Goddamn that shit hurt.

So how does one treat a gunshot wound to the leg?

I myself had to clean it twice a day while replacing bandages. I had a hole in the back of my calf where the bullet had entered. It was the size of my pinkie finger, and I had to pack it with gauze a good half inch deep. The exit wound in the front of my shin was a hole bigger than my thumb, and at least an inch deep. I had to clean and pack that with new gauze twice a day as well. That hurt like crazy – so thank god for the pain medication they gave me or else I don't know If I could have gone through with it. This went on for probably two months until it healed. Once healed I had a quarter-sized dimple scar that when I flexed my leg muscles it would look like it was winking. Talk about an ice breaker on the golf course, "So guys, anyone here ever been shot before?"

Not more than a month later I was back to work, trying to have some semblance of the reality I had before Halloween night. One Sunday night I was lying on the couch watching tv with my girlfriend, and I had the worst pain in my back – pain I had never felt before. It almost felt like I was going through these mini convulsions. My pain tolerance being pretty high at the time, I had no idea what was causing this. Did I pinch something by laying down awkward? Was it from having to crutch everywhere I went? I didn't know, but I did know that I was planning on going to work the next day. So I decided to take an extra pain pill and went to sleep.

The next day I was crutching down the stairs from my second story apartment and on through the parking lot. As I got closer to my car my breathing was more challenging than normal. I had let out a large cough only to find my tissue was covered in blood. This was bad. At the time I was a smoker, and thought holy shit you can cough up blood from smoking?! I called my doctor immediately and he said I had to rush down to the emergency room as they feared I had passed a blood clot.

Their fears were in-fact correct, that's exactly what had happened. I told them about all the pain I had the night before and they said that was the reason why. Shit man – I get shot, and a month later I'm coughing up blood. At this point I started to get a little worried. I understand that you cannot prescribe blood thinners to someone with an open wound in their leg, but they could have given me some fucking advanced notice right?! So for about a year I was on coumadin treatments. I would have to go to UC Davis Medical Center every Saturday morning to get my blood liquidity levels checked, which would determine the dosage of blood thinner I would be giving myself that week – every weekend for a year.

Fast forward a year later and I'm basically 95% recovered, able to enjoy my workouts and play sports with my friends again. I get asked to fill in at a company softball game – where I ended up breaking the same leg again taking a hard slide into second base. I was safe too, but only got tagged out when I keeled over writhing in pain. At least the guy that tagged me out had the decency to help me off the field. I ended up breaking my fibula in 4 places and tearing two ligaments clear off my ankle. I would end up having a plate, 10 screws, and a Kevlar band that rivaled the old Rector sets holding me back together. Then due to my history of blood clotting – I had to continue coumadin therapy for another full year – making those same weekly Saturday morning trips to get my levels checked – again.

But going back to just after the initial blood clots we were entering the holiday season and we started to get updates on the investigation into the shooters. I was in regular contact with the sheriff's homicide detectives and ultimately the district attorney trying those involved.

An update was given when we found out that one of the guys that had also gotten shot, his more severely going in through his stomach and exiting his back, was connected to the shooter. He was the shooter's cousin, and the sole reason for those guys being there that night in the first place. That was the missing link. He tried to maintain he didn't know who did it, and said if he did he wouldn't break the street code of snitching. Ultimately I think it was his grandmother that finally convinced him to come forward and identify his cousin as being one of those involved. This really set off the investigation that would gain traction quite quickly from then on.

The biggest break in the case was when, these stupid motherfuckers decided to take responsibility by posting it on Myspace – making it a federal crime which got the FBI involved. They were able to identify those involved, and during the raids of one of the homes – they were able to recover the girl's missing camera that had been stolen from the party that night. The camera all-telling, had pictures she had taken of her and her family followed by pictures the gang ended up taking of themselves which was totally incriminating.

It's funny how the street code is so against snitching until it's their ass on the line to take the fall, and how that credo crumbles when the only thing they can do to help themselves is to flip on the others. There were 7 guys at Patrick's house that night. I'd learn that five of them flipped on two main suspects, the shooter and the one that brought the gun to the party. They were charged with 1 count of Murder and 4 counts of attempted murder, my shot being one of those counts. I would end up testifying in court to what had happened that night. As I had maintained all along that I had no idea who they were, and weren't able to identify them that night. There was no way I could see the actual shooter shooting me because I was shot from behind. Ironically based on my testimony, my count of attempted murder was the only count not convicted on. The two were convicted of the count of Patrick's murder, 3 counts of attempted murder for the two guys that got shot in their arms, and the one shot in the stomach. There were also gun charges and gang enhancements. I cannot recall their exact sentence but they received like 90 years to life in prison, and would likely be dead by the time they would be first eligible for parole.

The trial would end up providing me with the closure that those involved were brought to justice. I would attend Patrick's funeral. Hearing his mother and father speak of their son's untimely death was heartbreaking. Thinking I very well could have been in his same situation, the thought of having to put my parents through what they had to endure made me appreciate life that much more, and would have an incredible impact on how I would conduct myself in the future.

As much as I thought I had mentally recovered, I hadn't. I wouldn't for quite some time. It took me years to seek out someone I could speak with about what had happened, and the residual impact it was having on me. I don't know if it was because I had my friends to talk to, or the fact that I so quickly immersed myself back into my career and achieving my life's goals that I didn't have the time for it. I think it certainly had a lot to do with the medication that I was on. I think that the medication was just a band aid to a wound that would seemingly never heal.

Over the next years to follow I would fall into an incredible depression. I had nightmares. My PTSD made it difficult for me to be in public places and in certain social situations. But at the time I had so much trust in that the medications I was on was the only thing that would help me cope and maintain any semblance of reality. But it ended up putting me in a state of mind that end up slowly unravelling everything I had worked so hard for and the relationships with those I had loved the most. I ended up losing my career, my house, my wife, my pride, and very much my sanity.

CHAPTER III.
PRESCRIPTIONS FIX EVERYTHING, RIGHT?

After experiencing something so traumatic, so randomly, for me it felt like my world had been flipped on its head. I should have sought counseling, however at the time my only goal was to continue on the path that I was on before all of this stuff went down. For lack of a better term, I really just put my head down and went back to work. I had an incredible support system, but they were not equipped to deal with what I had gone through.

Depression wasn't really on the forefront of my mind at the time. I think it was because everything had happened so quickly, most of my emotions were buried deep inside hoping they would just go away. Pushing aside my emotional pain, I was taking medication for the physical pain I was experiencing. Having to clean and dress my wounds twice daily, unravelling the blood-soaked gauze deep inside this crevasse that was the exit wound. I would clean and redress it for days that seemed like an eternity until it finally healed. That shit was painful. The aches at night would keep me up.

My PTSD was really bad when I was in large crowds or public places. Since being shot from behind, I had this extreme paranoia of what could be coming up behind me, thinking could something like this happen again? Standing in lines I grew uncomfortable with the short distance which people would stand next to me. I had certainly developed a personal bubble, and I didn't like how close random people would get. I had developed a means to cope with that unrest by standing sideways when waiting in line. Never did I stand normally in a single file line as the closeness for which people would be, especially from behind where I had no control over what was happening so close behind me. By standing sideways it gave me the ability to have more control over how close people would get. If people got too close I would shoot a murderous glare at them until they realized they needed to back off. Sometimes If I felt that my message wasn't getting across, I would 'bow up' or act like I was ready to fight them if they didn't. If they were too old, too young, or just too stupid to realize – I would explain to them that I had PTSD from being shot from behind, and that their close proximity to me was making me feel uncomfortable. I recall once going to the mall with my girlfriend not long after I was able to walk again. I am embarrassed to admit this, because now that I have kids of my own I realize how overreactive I was in certain places. That day at the mall was rough, as people would pace by, it was really unnerving. The worst example of this was at the mall that day. There was a group of teenage girls, doing nothing wrong other than being happy teenage girls. But there was a group of about four of them walking briskly arm in arm talking and laughing – as most teenage girls would do at the mall. The group was speeding up behind me, and based on the pace of the other mall walkers I didn't have anywhere to go – it felt like I was going to be run over. Not a proud moment for me, but I stopped, turned around and berated them with every cuss word imaginable. That would be a turning point for me, as I learned that this is not something wrong with everyone else so I thought, but something wrong with me. I was able to use the experience constructively, and would alter my behavior to be that much more accommodating to others in those situations. It is not uncommon still to this day to be walking, and if people were getting too close behind me, I would simply stop and let them pass.

A decade or so later we would have the onset of COVID-19, and the social distancing practices that came with during times of the pandemic. I loved this. This is what I wanted all along. Give me a few feet to feel like your not on top of me. It still irks me to see people what I call 'tailgating in line.' The line isn't going to move any quicker by you riding my ass. People can be really fucking inconsiderate in public sometimes.

I use to love to laugh and make others laugh, usually through some form of self-deprecating humor. However with me, there were certain situations that were off-limits. God help you if you snuck up on me, especially from behind. That quick element of surprise may be funny for some people, but not for me. There used to be a tv show with Bam Margera, a professional skateboarder on MTV. Part of the allure of the show was to watch Bam prank his parents, sneaking up on them in the dark, lighting firecrackers off at the foot of their bed when dead asleep. The parents' reaction sheer panic was part of what made the show so hilarious.

There were times that I thought I would literally be having a heart attack, where the instant shift of peace to panic was too much to bare. I never struck anyone, but when emotions are so high and so quickly altered, you have a choice of a reaction of fight or flight. I would joke with people like, "Hey don't be sneaking up on me unless you want to catch a hot one as a result. I throw elbows like Karl Malone."

By this time I still didn't feel the onset of depression to an extent that I asked for help. The anxiety I would experience didn't prompt me to ask for help either, I just felt like it was behavior that I would have to learn to control. The only medication I would end up taking regularly was Ambien. Ambien ended up ruining my life.

I did have nightmares for the first few months, so getting a restful night's sleep was certainly a challenge. Ambien was a sure thing. At first I could take an Ambien and be asleep in minutes, and have a restful 6 hours of uninterrupted sleep. A huge fear of mine was to not be able to perform my job to the best of my abilities and the expectations placed upon me. Without Ambien, my mind would literally race the entire night. I'd replay every event that happened in my life and the things I could have done differently. I would think and think and think until daybreak unless I had taken something to sleep.

I never abused Ambien. It was prescribed to me by my doctor from the time I was shot in 2008, until the time I enrolled myself into rehab in 2016. I know that prescription drug abuse was certainly something that I could fall into, however I never used or abused Ambien as a party drug. I would be given my prescribed dosage for the month as covered by my health insurance. I did not seek out dirty doctors for additional pills, even when I felt I needed more because I had grown such a tolerance throughout the years.

I had travelled for work, canvasing the United States from 2011 to 2016. I was a travelling salesman of sorts, and for the first 2 and a half years I covered a territory of 36 states, basically everything outside of the northeast and southeast. I would consult Financial Advisors and Insurance Agents on Mutual Fund investing for their clients, and often gave hour-long continuing education seminars to groups in the hundreds. It was not uncommon for me to fly to one state on a Sunday, driving through that state and others until Friday when I would fly back home from an airport hundreds of miles from where I started. Often I would fly to different time zones, which would make it incredibly difficult to acclimate immediately. Traveling from the west coast to the east coast was so challenging for me, especially considering I wasn't much of a morning person to begin with. When working on the east coast I would often have my first meetings of the morning at 8:00 am local time, but as far as my body clock was concerned it still felt like 5:00 am – and that's not when I had to wake up but when I had to be there. I was a presenter, a public speaker, and when speaking in front of large audiences you have to have confidence. If you have ever seen someone stumble or fumbling on stage, sweating profusely, I have been there. These were some of the obstacles I had to overcome through a ton of practice, which built up my confidence. But if you're presenting to a group of people and you're running on fumes because you only got so many hours of sleep the night before due to the time change – that would certainly impact your performance.

The reason I continued to take Ambien regularly, long after many of the reasons I was taking it for post-shooting stress, was for the convenience. I could fly to the east coast on a red-eye, pop an Ambien and get 5 hours of restful sleep on the plane to be in a position confident enough to go live on stage as soon as I arrived.

My primary care physician and I had a great relationship. I felt like he listened to my concerns and gave me his best to remedy. Since the shooting I was prescribed pain medication. I knew of how easy it was to become addicted. At the time I loved the feeling it gave me, I was pain-free, it was everything I had wanted at the time. My doctor and I had a discussion about that very concern and it was agreed that not too long after my wounds had healed, and the most difficult part of physical rehab was over, that I no longer needed pain medication. We agreed, and there was no issue. If I had pain thereafter, it was nothing that couldn't be relieved by a Tylenol or Ibuprofen.

I still struggle with why we didn't have that same conversation when it came to Ambien. I was prescribed this for 8 years. Never once did the conversation turn to the fact that this also was a heavily addictive drug. We never planned a weening off process. There was never a line in the sand, similar to the pain medication, where my doctor refused to prescribe. If there was, it certainly was not compelling enough to stop. To my own fault I did find myself in a position where I could almost manipulate the conversation away from getting to that point.

What had ultimately transpired after 8 years of taking Ambien daily was that I no longer could have the restful 6 hours of sleep ready for whatever the next day would bring me. I had built up so much of a tolerance that I could only get in reality 2-3 hours, and then I would be wide awake. This put me in a sort of a zombie state of mind, where I was no longer the quick-witted snarky joke-making people-pleaser, I was a mess.

At this point I had everything anyone could want. I was making a great income for someone in their mid-twenties. I had bought a nice house in an affluent neighborhood with a pool that had a slide. The bocci ball court had an overhanging trellis with what looked like grape vines woven through. We had a built-in firepit and an exterior office where I could work from home when not on the road. We had a beautiful baby boy and we would soon welcome to the world my vibrant and spunky daughter. My wife at the time didn't have to work, and so she had everything she wanted in life.

Like Biggie Smalls most famous quote, 'The more money you have, the more problems you get,' certainly has some truth to it. Can money buy happiness? Shit – I'm sure if you had enough of it you could certainly find a way. Money didn't buy happiness for me, but it certainly provided peace of mind. I had enough to pay my bills, save some for retirement, and still have plenty discretionary spending to enjoy the free time we had.

Despite having a great career with one of the best companies anyone could wish to work for, there was a ceiling as far as advancement opportunities once I had gotten to a certain point. I was being recruited by a much smaller firm out of Chicago to represent them in their west coast territory. At the time I had grown tired of the mileage I was putting on myself. It had become quite tiresome travelling throughout the country.

Living in the Sacramento region and flying out of SMF - Sacramento International Airport, there typically were no direct flights east of Denver. I was a loyal Southwest Airlines customer, due to the volume of flights that went in and out of SMF at the time. Delta airlines always found a way to cancel my flight, and United had lost my bags, so Southwest being that they never fucked me over was my best option. However in doing so, many of my flights had at least 1 stop, some more. So when it came to flying as far as I did, it would basically eat an entire day getting there and another day getting back.

My decision to leave wasn't for greed. It wasn't for the massive influx in income, as for the most part it would end up being comparable, however it was certainly not the amount that was promised to me during their courtship. The position would be exclusively working in regions close to home in areas I was familiar with. Instead of 37 states as a territory, I covered a geography of Fresno, CA to Anchorage, AK – and everywhere in between. Everywhere I went, with the seldom exclusion of Alaska, was a direct flight away, and many times there were options every hour or two.

I had accepted the new role and loved my title of Regional Vice President. The most critical error I had made, which would have a tremendous impact on my quality of life thereafter, was that I didn't get everything in writing. Handshake deals are great if you value the person extending their hand to you, but in business – get everything in writing.

Being new to a sales territory, I had no idea of what kind of sales I would make in the early period of reestablishing and creating new relationships. It is customary to ask for a guarantee on sales, a minimum compensation regardless of what sales were made, to give me the peace of mind knowing I would be able to cover my living expenses until I was able to build a territory. The company had balked at my request for a guarantee, which made me incredibly reluctant. However they did offer to share with me the trailing 12-month's sales, and asked that if those numbers were greater than the guarantee I had asked for, would I be willing to accept. Unfortunately I took them for their word, however their word turned out to be shit. I would find out after just a week of onboarding that the previous 12-month's sales they had shown me, under the premise that those numbers would continue, were in fact no longer attainable. The week I had started our biggest client at the time had purchased a competitor of ours, lowered their management fee to an extent there was no way we could remain competitive, and incentivized their Advisors to sell their newly proprietary investment over ours.

Talk about putting faith in others and then getting kicked in the balls for trusting in their ability to be honest. Fuck – I should've not walked away at that time, but ran. Ran like my hair was on fire. But no, I was a prideful fucker and I couldn't bring myself to go back to my previous company as a result. I ended up staying with the company for 2 and a half years - 2 and a half years too long. The distrust had permeated my attitude towards management to what I could only describe as disdain.

Psychologically I felt like I was losing my mind, losing my grip with the reality that I would soon lose everything as a result. They certainly had played a big part in my demise, and for years I had the most violent thoughts for the one that had lied to me. I can't blame everything on them though. I wasn't sleeping. I remember one day I had meetings at a major brokerage firm in Modesto, Ca. That's when I had my first panic attack. I had gone to Panera Bread to buy breakfast for the entire staff, and then I'd walk-through the office meeting with Advisors in 10-15 minute increments, where I had the opportunity to position the investments the company I represented could manage on behalf of their clients.

I had done this for years. I felt no pressure going into the situation, as I had conducted similar meetings in much more high stress environments. But this day was different. I felt like I literally lost all confidence I had in just a few moments sitting down with this gentleman. What happened next was something that looked like it could only have come out of a movie. I started sweating profusely. Like really fucking bad. I had always kept a handkerchief, but ten handkerchiefs wouldn't have been able to soak up all of the sweat. On top of that, I was wearing a light blue collared shirt – that very quickly turned dark. I had to apologize and quickly exit the meeting, as I couldn't stand embarrassing myself any further.

The next week I had met with my doctor and explained what had happened. At the time I was willing to try anything, as my livelihood was at stake. If I couldn't get my shit together, and quick, this was certainly going to make it's way back to Chicago, and then I would have been really fucked. So my doctor prescribed me Benzodiazepine, generic for Xanax.

That was my magic bullet! Xanax cured everything. I could take one before going into the office, and I was like my old self again. I was able to focus, hold articulate conversations, and everything seemed like it was heading in the right direction. I did not abuse the drug, but I did take it daily. I think the prescription bottle said something to the effect of take one as needed. Well I had to work 5 days a week, and the other two were spent doting my two babies and trying to be a supportive husband, so as needed for me was every day. This went on for maybe 3 months. But with my dependence of Ambien, only getting 2 hours of sleep per night, using Xanax was really like using a band aid when you need stitches.

I would end up getting fired for job abandonment, as after a while I just couldn't represent the company in good conscience. At that point I had already lost everything. I had a hard time looking at myself in the mirror and being proud of the person looking back at me. My marriage was deteriorating, money was now tight, and quality of life cutbacks weren't really acceptable at that time. We decided to sell the house to downsize, something that was and still is heartbreaking for me to think of. The only way I could think of salvaging my life at that time was to admit myself to a drug rehabilitation facility. Boy was that a shit show...

CHAPTER IV. REHAB

When you think you're losing your mind, there's probably some truth to that. March 3rd, 2016, was the day I decided to try and get it back. I knew I couldn't do it alone. I needed help desperately. My life was in complete shambles. I had fucked so many good things up, I didn't have much left. I was so embarrassed at my precipitous downward spiral, I didn't want anyone to see it. Outside of my immediate family, I turned into a bit of a social recluse. I was so ashamed of myself losing everything I worked so hard for, I had a hard time making eye-contact with people. This coming from someone that just years prior thrived in social engagements, being comfortable speaking in front of dozens of people on stage for sometimes an hour at a time. I had lost my confidence. I didn't really know who to turn to. My family was and still is my strongest support system, but they weren't equipped to deal with me in the state of mind I was in.

That was the day I decided to check myself into a Treatment facility located in Orange County. I had done my research, and decided I didn't want to go somewhere too close to home. I viewed rehab as a place that I could go to that was away from home, get better, and leave that experience behind me hundreds of miles away.

I had no idea of what to expect. I knew I wasn't going to Passages Malibu, so being driven around in Range Rovers to get my nails done was certainly not going to happen. But I ended up at a facility that was smack dab in the middle of the hood. I arrived via one of the last flights of the night. It was late, and I had never been to this part of Orange County. We certainly weren't close to any sandy beaches that's for damn sure. But I arrived with an open mind, and a desire to get better. I had so much to lose, I couldn't afford not to.

I had been picked up at the airport by one of the counselors, and we arrived at what looked like a small apartment complex. As soon as you walked in, there was the men's quarters on the right, women's quarters on the left. In between those living quarters there were 2 buildings, one was an office with a group therapy room and the laundry room just behind it. The other building was the kitchen and cafeteria. In the center of all of these buildings was a courtyard with patio tables and chairs.

I remember walking through the corridor with my bags towards the office, and they must have heard that there was someone new arriving, because there was a large group having a smoke break welcoming me in. I kinda felt like fresh meat, with all eyes on me trying to size up who I was and what I was in for. I had never been to rehab before. I didn't know who I was going to be staying with, or what to really expect while I was there. It wasn't like jail, I'd never been so I couldn't tell you firsthand. It certainly had some vibes consistent with what I would imagine things are like there though. The best description I could give is that it felt like a group home for adults.

During my initial check-in they had me unpack all my belongings onto the floor for them to check for anything illegal or against the rules. They took my Gillette Razor and held on to it until I would check it out to shave, and then I had to return it back to them. I didn't know the reason why I couldn't have a shaving razor was because someone might try to kill themselves with it. That was something new that was made abundantly clear. They also took my hand sanitizer as well. They said desperate alcoholics would end up drinking anything with alcohol in it to get their fix. At that point I started to realize the gravity of the situation I put myself in.

They took my medication, and we talked about going to a doctor the next day to receive my new drug protocols that they'd put me on as I detoxed. I had only made plans to be there for a few weeks. They would then explain to me that there were 3 types of substance abuses that if you didn't detox properly, you could die. Those three were Alcohol, Ambien, and Benzodiazepines. I was addicted to 2 of the 3, as I never had a problem with drinking. Hard alcohol in excess always gave me the worst headaches and hangovers. In college I could very well drink a 12-pack of Coors Lights with my buddies if the occasion called for it. But I wasn't an alcoholic, as I could go weeks without drinking without issue.

This is when they told me that I would probably need to stay there for at least 3 months. After 3 months of counseling and proper detox, they felt I would be ready to go back home.

"3 fucking months?!" I thought to myself. I've got babies at home I needed to bond with. I can't say that I immediately agreed to that duration of stay, but I was starting to come to grips with it. As it would turn out I would only last 11 days.

Cell phones were forbidden upon arrival until 5 days had gone by. I also didn't realize this was because people in rehab would use them to get drugs delivered to them. Not having my cell phone was a huge sacrifice. I couldn't call or text my family. I couldn't check the scores and sports news I had made a habit of throughout my day. Any connection to the outside world I had to give up for that period of time, and that was a tough pill to swallow – pun intended.

The first night I was there they showed me to my room. There were 4 rooms in the men's quarters, 2 beds per room. There was a bathroom with a shower, and a common area family room that had couches and a big screen TV. Ironically the night I arrived everyone was watching The Walking Dead, what a fucking metaphor for the experience I was about to have!

It was late and we had to start the morning at 8:00 am for what they called morning meditation – which wasn't meditation at all - more like reading from the Alcoholics Anonymous book and discussed how that related to our experiences. So I ended up going straight to bed. I didn't get to meet my roommate, as he was sound asleep. They had taken my Ambien from me during check-in, so

I couldn't sleep. I quickly learned that the Counselor covering the night shift would open the door every hour to check to make sure you were still there and not up to no good. I'd lay there in the dark, my mind racing about everything I had gotten myself into – If I was counting sheep I would have been in the thousands by day break. But like clockwork, every hour the door would open up with the piercing light shining through, as he'd poke his head in to check if I was still there. "Yes motherfucker I'm still here," I thought to myself, and there's no way I am going to be able to sleep now being interrupted like that. He would end up being really cool in the end though.

So unbeknownst to me, my roommate was in a pretty severe state of detox. My sinuses were stuffed up the whole night as they always had the heater going like 80 degrees at night – so my sense of smell was shot. Turns out this guy was blowing the room up with farts all night, and the next day my introduction to the group came with a fresh set of pink eye – what a fucking mess.

My roommate and I ended up getting to know each other pretty well by the end of my stay. He was in his 50's, but the toll alcoholism took on him made him look like he was in his 70's or 80's. His story was that he would drink a 5th of Vodka with a fist full of Vicodin every day, until it got to the point where he went to the emergency room and they told him that if he had another sip of Vodka his esophagus would explode. Talk about a 'come to Jesus' moment.

My first day at Treatment was tough. I woke up with Pink Eye, I hadn't slept, and I felt like I was in a worse-off state than before I arrived. I got to meet everyone though – that was cool. There was a bit of comradery in that we were all there for the same reason, but you could tell that not everyone had the sincere intention of wanting to get better, almost like they were just going through the motions.

There weren't many women, maybe 2 or 3. There was always a female counselor chaperoning their living quarters as I guess they had a history of getting into trouble. The one I remember the most, she was sweet to everyone. I remember a few times she made out with some of the guys there on separate occasions, which was considered a 'violation', which is why I think she was monitored as much as she was.

Her story was interesting as she was kind of a celebrity there. She had been in and out of the facility, which seemed like it wasn't for the purpose of recovering. Moreso a detox place she would hang out at until she got bored, and then she'd leave and relapse, and the cycle repeated. She was one of two people there that were Native American from the Palm Springs area. I think she was half-Mexican, but the other half qualified her for tribal income. So here I was in the Financial Services Industry, with a career that generated a good income – and she was receiving like $10,000+ per month from her tribe's casinos. Her problem was that she didn't know how to behave responsibly with that amount of guaranteed disposable income, and would often buy Meth and get into trouble with gangs. The type of stuff that would end you up in rehab. For her it was almost like a vacation spot. Luckily I would stay in touch with her for a few years after I left through Snapchat. She ended up having a baby, and I think that put her in the right perspective.

The other resident that had been receiving tribal money had a very similar approach. He would come to treatment and detox for a few weeks, then leave for a Meth binge, only to come back and repeat that cycle all over again. For me being someone that had to go to college, and study for licenses and certifications in order to make that type of living it was hard to conceptualize. I kept thinking to myself the positive things I could do with that money – but they didn't have that mindset. Why would they invest it if they could just spend it on an opulent lifestyle, which to them justified their spending habits. He and I got along well despite his imposing stature and cranky attitude at times. He would end up having a run in with some of the other guys there that was for me insane to think about, but it happened.

For me I just tried to be friends with everybody, but my behavior in detox was not everyone's cup of tea. There were at least 2 guys there that didn't like me and they made it known. During the first week I was getting acclimated to the drug protocols they had put me on to detox from the Ambien and Xanax, there were 9 prescriptions total. During which time I was happy, in a bit of a state of bliss. I had a habit of talking way too much and way too fast, and I could understand why the other two guys didn't like me. One guy just thought I was annoying as fuck, and would tell me often. He was a grizzled biker-type guy in his early 50's or so. He was there for his addiction to Meth. He would tell us about time he spent in prison when he was in Alabama. Most of it may have been just talk, but he was a pretty scary guy, and not someone I particularly wanted to be on his bad side. He never threatened me outright, he would more so say things jokingly. One day we were in morning meditation, and he made a comment to me in front of everyone there that he was going to stab me with a spoon. We all kind of laughed, because we didn't really think he was going to attack me – that was just his way of telling me to shut up. The counselor though had taken it really seriously and made a big deal about it. I guess in his way of stepping in and bringing attention to it, the guy ended up lightening up a bit. I would go over afterwards and apologize because in the state of mind I was in, I was acting a little bonkers myself and realized how annoying I could be to someone that didn't know me. He and I would end up being friends. We had gone on a beach day to Laguna Beach, and before we left I let him borrow one of my tank tops, and that seemed to be the olive branch we needed.

The other guy that didn't like me I think was more because I was misunderstood. He was homeless before he had come to treatment, and had experienced things living on the streets of Los Angeles that I could've never imagined. I think it was a bit of a culture shock, as here I came in a white guy that was well-off and that contrast at first was pretty tough for him. We would end up being pretty cool with each other by the end of my stay. I gave him his space because you could tell he was more accustomed to being alone and preferred being more in his own bubble per se. I'll never forget how he looked exactly like the 90's R&B singer Maxwell. I hope he ended up okay, he showed a lot of promise.

While in treatment I developed a pretty strong bond with two other guys there. They were both 5-10 years younger than I was at that time, and I kind of felt a responsibility to watch out for them. In many ways they reminded me of myself, and I couldn't help but feel they looked up to me as a friend but also a mentor. I specifically came to rehab for the sole purpose of getting my mind right and my life back on track – not to fuck around and dig myself deeper into the hole I was already in. But that wasn't the overarching theme there. I had so much to live for being a young father. I saw so much potential in these guys in getting their shit together too. They were still so young in my eyes, they had the rest of their adult lives ahead of them, it kind of felt like in school that there should be no child left behind. There's a South Park episode where they talked about the 'Accountabilibuddy,' a friend that held you accountable. Even in the mental disarray I was in at the time, my moral compass was always there with me. It was the only right thing to do, and in many ways, they helped me as much as I helped them.

They came from loving and supportive families, just like I did. They were smart, well-educated, but there is no socioeconomic status that is immune to addiction. I think how they fell into drugs was the same way a lot of young people do. You try it out with your friends because it's seen as the cool thing to do because they do it. Then that occurrence turns into a pattern, then it becomes a habit, until ultimately you are fully addicted. One of them was addicted to Xanax, or 'bars' as he called them. He said he started by taking them from his aunt's medicine cabinet. That turned into buying them on the street, and by the time he was in rehab he was taking up to 6 or 7 doses per day. My other friend told me stories of how easy it was to buy drugs on the internet, the dark web as he referred to it as. It was like buying something on Amazon today. You comb through the menu of options. You search, you'd get to decide what kind, the quantity, and how fast you wanted it to get there, and a few days later he'd get a package in the mail. I thought this was absolutely nuts, how are these guys not getting caught?! Back then these activities still fell under the radar of law enforcement. I would've been so paranoid. Like all of a sudden you're checking your mail and a group of FBI agents come out of nowhere and you're busted, but that never happened to him. However it was the ease and frequency for which he had access to his fix that perpetuated his addiction into what it had become.

Just like in the movie Blow, when Boston George goes to prison with a diploma in Pot and came out with a PhD in Cocaine – that was very much what I was experiencing at the time. Meth and Heroin were dirty drugs to me, where if you got hooked the process of recovering was not in your favor. I would have never in a million years thought I would be making friends with people that were into that shit – but that was what rehab was all about. People were powerless over their addictions no matter what they were into, and they needed help just the same.

A major theme for recovery in treatment was admitting that you were powerless over your addiction. In some cases it was the habit of partying that kept it going, for most thereafter it was to continue the habit for fear of withdrawals, what they would call getting 'dope sick.' For me it was how I was able to function as a semi-responsible adult professional, with the burden of being the sole bread winner of the family. I can't make excuses for what happened, but for me that was a tremendous amount of pressure. If Ambien and Xanax were things that I could've quit cold-turkey, I would've done so. I had kicked smoking cigarettes before that way. Yeah, I was a cranky dickhead for a few days. I would chew gum like I was Pete Carroll to take my mind off of it. This time was different though. This time I had help, and I didn't have to do it alone. But like I said, not everyone there had the honest intentions of getting better. The night shit went down would be the personification of just that.

This was probably my 5th or 6th night in rehab. The eye drops they gave me had cured my pink eye, and the drug regiment they had me on had finally allowed me to have my first great night's sleep. I remember that day well to because it was also the first day I was allowed off campus. I had never been in a situation where I had basically all but given up my right to leave. I was confined. Though I believed in my treatment and the protocols they had in place, it still sucked not to have the freedom to go to the 7-Eleven with everybody else. Every day we would go on a field trip per se, walking the half mile or so to the local convenient store. People would buy snacks, candy, sodas, cigarettes, for me it was chewing tobacco. Up until that day I had to give cash to one of my friends to go grab something at the store for me.

This day I had a special request though. I wanted a haircut. Not just because my neckline had started to get out of hand, but it was much more of an intimate experience for me, almost like a cleansing. I was able to convince one of the counselors to take me, but I brought along one of my friends too. He was in need of one as well, but for him it wasn't so much about the haircut as it was this experience of earned freedom. Almost like we were in jail, and someone asked us what would be the first thing we'd do when we'd get out. We were going to get a haircut, symbolism of the new us, the cleansed us. I would never have thought going and getting a haircut with someone would be such a bonding experience, but for us it had much more meaning than that, a transformation of sorts. A symbol of the good times ahead.

That same day though, when we got back there was a different vibe amongst the others, almost like something went down while we were gone, or something was about to go down. You'd be hanging out talking to someone, and then you'd see others in the distance kind of whispering secretly. They were making plans. These plans I would later find out were that some of the guys were getting drugs snuck into the facility that night. Of course when

I heard this my moral compass is ringing alarms in my head. It was like in the old Looney Tunes shows where you'd see a cartoon angel on one side of the shoulder, and the devil on the other. Both were giving conflicting advice. I knew that this was wrong, but I didn't feel like it was my place at the time to say anything. I didn't want to be labeled a snitch, and in that controlled environment, there was nowhere to go if I had. If I had blown the whistle, there was no telling what these guys would do to me. I could handle them one on one, but all 4 of them at once, that wasn't a risk I was willing to take.

That night we had dinner and most of us would hang out in the courtyard, listen to music, talk about life on the outside. Some were in the men's quarters watching a movie. That night I was exhausted, so it would turn out to be the best night sleep I had in over a week. By that time I had basically forgot about all of the rumblings earlier in the day, and I went straight to bed. I must've slept for like 10 hours. Those every hour bed checks that the overnight counselor would be responsible for, I had slept right through them. I woke up feeling great, like a renewed self. My roommates had a habit of turning the heat up at night to like 80 degrees, so when I got up I was drenched in sweat. My clothes, my sheets, my pillow were all soaked. It was like I had wet the bed the night before. I didn't care though, I was stoked I finally slept. I would later do laundry and wash my sheets. To air the room out I opened up the window and placed my wet pillow on the windowsill to dry out in the sunlight.

It was maybe 7:00 am, way earlier than the times my roommates typically got up. We were basically free to go to bed when we wanted, so a lot of us would stay up super late, and sleep in just until the point we had to be up for morning meditation. The facility had this old 1980's weight set in the garage that looked like it hadn't been used in years, and that morning I had gotten up to get some exercise. I was totally aloof to what was going on, and briefly had forgotten what everyone was up in arms about the night before. I had slept like a rock, so I was completely oblivious.

I stroll out of my room as I make my way through the common area to the front door and on to the garage. As I'm walking through, I notice a bunch of my roommates on the couch watching a movie. I had no idea, I had thought maybe they got up early too and decided to get some Netflix in. I casually greet them with a good morning, and even asked if they wanted to join me in the garage to lift weights. They seemed fixed to couch intent on watching what they were, and I knew they wouldn't join me, but that was my mood that morning. I was happy, energized, and excited for what the day would have in store. Turns out that day would have a lot in store, one of the most memorable moments I would have in my time there.

I went about my workout. I took a shower, had my coffee and breakfast. I would greet everyone with a gracious good morning and a smile that I was told was infectious. We had our morning meditation, which again would consist of reading verses from the Alcoholics Anonymous book and then a roundtable discussion on the topic and how it related to us and our journey. Not everyone was there though. The guys that were watching tv when I woke up, I guess they went to bed and so it was a lite group. We would finish up. Some people would get their morning medication and get cleaned up for the day. I had gotten a head start on everyone that morning so I was more in observation mode at that point.

Things then started to get pretty tense, and the vibe had certainly shifted. I could tell something was going on because all of the counselors had a brief meeting together, and then they all fanned out and started rounding everyone up. Everyone had to come out into the courtyard. The manager of the facility was there, and I hadn't met him yet. I would later find out that he normally wasn't there unless something bad had happened. While they had everyone in the courtyard, some of the counselors and the manager were tossing rooms, checking to see if there were any drugs that made their way in the night before.

This is when all of the previous day's rumblings started to come back to me. Looking around at everyone huddled up on the patio, you could tell something wasn't right. Some of the guys looked pretty nervous. That's when I learned that all of the talks about getting drugs in the day prior was in fact successful the night before.

They brought one of the younger guys out, he was maybe 19 or 20. He had all of his stuff packed with his guitar and he was arguing with the manager about getting kicked out. I guess this wasn't the first time he would be kicked out of a rehab, and he was pretty distraught at the thought of how his parents would react. He didn't go peacefully, and there was certainly the tension that he wasn't going to go without a fight. Turns out he was the guy that had orchestrated getting the drugs in that night. He was a local kid and was able to arrange a delivery during a period when the night counselor wasn't making his rounds. I think they did raise some suspicion, which ultimately led to them getting caught.

I was outside in a state of awe. I was like, what the fuck is going on here?! I thought - Isn't this the place where people go to get off drugs – not bring them in?!? As I'm observing, and trying to take this all in. The manager came out and yelled, "Who's fucking pillow is propped up in the window?" He was in fact referring to my pillow, that I had put there to dry after sweating so much the night before. I explained it to him just like that right then and there. Thinking, well what do you expect me to do , put it in the dryer that everyone else uses to dry their clean clothes with?! He shot back, "You know what that looks like to me? It looks like something you would put there to sneak out of the window to get drugs!" I had no other way of responding other than the snarky reply of, "Well that would make a whole lot of sense if you had sensitive knees." Everyone laughed but him. He initially had thought I was involved but clearly I didn't know what the fuck happened, and after talking with the other counselors I was cleared. When he was leaving for the day I made sure to introduce myself. He was a short guy, a real Napoleonic type. I made sure to leave him with, "I expected you to be a lot shorter."

So one guy was getting kicked out, and everyone was now aware of what had happened, at least from a high level perspective. We were all immediately ordered to take a U.A. or Urine Analysis. I guess this was the way they could tell who had been using the night before and those who hadn't. I came out in the clear and was sent on my way. One by one they'd call people in and have them pee in a cup, they'd test it in front of them, and if they were like me they were able to go about their day. This process made me feel pretty damn uncomfortable, so I decided to make myself busy by cleaning my sheets with a load of laundry.

I noticed my two closest friends were not doing too great. They had looked so nervous, that is when I found out that they were also a part of this, which was really disappointing for me. They decided to be upfront with the staff prior to taking their urine test, that they had partaken and remorseful for what they had done. By being truthful about what they had done, they were given a second chance and were allowed to stay. There was another guy there that had put in for some of the drugs, but ended up not getting any to use. I don't know if he was ever implicated, but he was there that night.

So as the day unfolded, more and more of the story started to come out. I was dead asleep when all of this was going down, in the room next door just a few feet from where I was sleeping.

As it would happen, the local guy was able to get his connect to come to the facility to make the drop-off. He had made the arrangements, and when they had the opportunity in between the night counselor's rounds they were able to make it happen. They had ordered Meth and Heroin. They didn't have a way to ingest it, and I guess they had looked for something they could smoke it out of. This is where the story got a lot more interesting for me. I would learn that they would steal a 'pipe' from the Giant Native American guy to smoke it. I guess he had a makeshift pipe that he fashioned out of a light bulb. But he still had some of his meth in their saved, so when he found out they had taken it and smoked his meth too, he was pissed. He would then bust through the door of the room these 4 guys were getting high in with a violent rage. He came in with a tube sock he had stuffed a bunch of rocks in, and was swinging it around like one of those medieval times ball and chain Melee weapons. I could only imagine their reaction when this giant of a man stormed through the door to collect what they had stolen from him. It was now gone and you had to defend yourself from this guy swinging a sock full of rocks?! Somehow they were able to get the guy to calm down, and no one was hurt, but I think that was what had alerted staff to what had happened. I'm not an expert on the half-life of methamphetamine in one's system, and I don't know how recent he had gotten high, but when everyone was drug tested he wasn't one that had come up positive.

Some crazy shit right?! The saddest part of it was that my two closest friends had been caught up in this, and both ended up doing meth for the first time. That was pretty disappointing to me. No wonder these guys were up watching tv at 7:00 am and didn't want to go work out with me, they were high on meth from the night before!

As part of my treatment program the Psychologist on staff had made me take The Minnesota Multiphasic Personality Inventory (MMPI) exam. This was a questionnaire of sorts with hundreds of questions, most of which were forms of repeated questions asked prior. He would use the results of this exam to diagnose me as suffering from Bipolar Disorder with PTSD. This was the first time I was told I was mentally ill. I didn't want to agree with it at first. I likened it initially to having multiple personality disorder, and that was far from how I had viewed myself. Over time it started to make more and more sense though. I had the most difficult time controlling my emotions. Not so much that a switch could be flipped and I would immediately shift from one emotion to the other, but more so that I couldn't control the level of highs and lows. Those highs and lows certainly put me in sometimes a manic state, sometimes depressive. This to me did make sense. As I was continuing my treatment, with the vast volume of prescription drug protocols they'd have me on, my family members bared witness to my state of mania. Those were some of the most regretful experiences in my life. I was absolutely bonkers. I had no sense of reason. I remember back on my behavior then and it was the most embarrassing and shameful time of my life.

I lasted 11 days at the rehab facility in Orange County. My last days there, the staff had not gotten my prescriptions refilled in time, and there were two days where I didn't have the medication they would give me to help me sleep. The last night I was a bit delirious as a result. I told the overnight staff that I would be awake all night in what I termed a sleep strike. All I wanted was to get sleep, to rest that weary mind of mine. But I decided to make a stink about it, act pretty obnoxiously with staff, packed my bags and left. I called a cab at like 3:00 am, and had them drop me off at (SNA) John Wayne airport. I would pace frantically outside the airport for like 3 and a half hours until I could catch the first flight back home.

Upon my arrival I clearly understood the gravity of the situation, and mentally I was in really bad shape. I had left treatment in under 2 weeks, when they had told me originally that I would need to stay up to 3 months to properly detox.

The weeks following would prove to be the most stressful and straining for those relationships I had so close to me. Deep down I still had a desire to get better, but I refused to seek additional treatment. By the time I had gotten back, my parents were helping me get into another treatment center closer to home. We arrived and I was open to it, but I had to wait for hours as they waited for the approval from my insurance company, whom at the time thought I was still in treatment in Orange County. That wait for whatever reason was too much for me, and I stormed out of there. This place was in a nice residential community, and I had got into an argument with my dad about how I didn't want to go there. My behavior was so out of character, I had said some really mean things to my dad, things I horribly regretted. I made them leave, and told them to drive the 2 hours back to their home. I somehow made my way back to my house at the time. A few days later I would agree to go to a center in Sonoma County, close to where my parents were. This place was serene and peaceful, everyone was very welcoming, and it would have been a good place for me. Mentally, I wasn't in a capacity to go along with their rules. I didn't want to surrender my cell phone for a week, and I missed my kids terribly. Not after just a few hours of getting dropped off and going through intake, I up and decided fuck this place I'm out of here. I called a cab and they picked me up on this dirt road out in the country and took me to a hotel in town. I'd end up spending the night and taking a bus back home to Sacramento the next morning. This really put a strain on my relationship with my parents. I have the best parents, they never deserved this treatment, I would be forever remorseful for those few weeks.

When I got back to Sacramento I still had the strong desire to get better, but I wasn't going back to any treatment facility. I worked closely with a new doctor that helped me follow the protocols I needed to get back into the headspace I so much desired. I would end up a loyal follower of the AA program. I went to Alcoholics Anonymous meetings, Narcotics Anonymous meetings as well. Sometimes I'd attend 2 or 3 per day. My sobriety then was incredibly important to my recovery. I ended up being sober for over a year. NA and AA had really helped me recover. I didn't follow the steps as I should have. I had a great sponsor that I could identify with as he was a businessman like I was. The reason I decided to no longer follow the steps and teachings, was that I had a really hard time admitting that I was an Addict and an Alcoholic.

The first step of the AA and NA program is the realization that I was powerless over my addiction and that I needed help. But my addiction was really just a function of the medication I was on at the time of my shooting, and was too ignorant to realize the negative long term impacts it would have on me. So when I would attend a meeting, and everyone would stand up and introduce themselves followed by stating they're an addict or alcoholic. There wasn't all that much truth to my statement. I didn't have a problem with alcohol, so to say I was an alcoholic was in fact a fallacy. When stating I was an addict, that wasn't in my mind entirely true either. The only things I was addicted to, I had no idea I was addicted in the first place. These were not drugs of pleasure and party. They were drugs that could be abused, but I took them as prescribed. In my opinion, I wouldn't have been going to rehab in the first place if the correct medical advice was given to me way long before it had become an everyday part of my life. I leaned more heavily on family support. I turned to athletics, becoming a gym rat of sorts. I had found the best therapist I would talk to candidly about everything that troubled me in life, and she was a total godsend in empowering me to make positive changes on my behalf. I couldn't have recovered without those resources. Was it the right way to go about it – maybe or maybe not. Despite my hellish relationship with rehab and drug treatment centers, I was still able to recover on my terms and It proved successful.

CHAPTER V. WATER FROM A ROCK

How do you get water from a rock? I've always loved that saying. To me it meant that you can't get something from which it doesn't have. That was my financial situation in a nutshell. This was an incredible struggle for me for years. I had gone bankrupt when credit cards I had accumulated prior to keep my family afloat had mounted so overwhelmingly that I couldn't make the monthly interest payments. I had no way of paying those off. I was divorced, I had lost the ability to earn even the most minimal living within the industry that I thought I loved. It's tough getting a job as a Financial Advisor when you have a bankruptcy on your record, which makes a lot of sense from the consumer point of view. I have a degree in Finance and a decade's experience consulting Financial Advisors. I was more than qualified.

Through exuding my passion for helping people make the best-informed decisions on behalf of their investments, I was able to win over management and sign on with a major bank in the region to offer my services. The income was more than half of what I was making in my previous position, but I still had the bills that came with my previously higher salary. I had credit card bills, my student loan, a car payment for the most modest of vehicles. I had to pay rent, utilities, car insurance, health insurance for my kids, life insurance in case I passed away, child support, and the list goes on and on.

I didn't stand a chance. Any income I was making was still falling well short of what I needed to keep myself afloat. I had to make drastic changes to my lifestyle, which wasn't one of opulence prior to, but I was comfortable. Me being a Financial Advisor didn't take long to realize that I had a serious cash flow problem. I looked at every expenditure I had on the ledger, and cut back as much as I could to the most barest of essentials. I was still falling short. If it came to a bill, I would pay that bill even if it meant I wasn't going to eat. I had developed an eating disorder. People would say, "Justin you look great, what are you doing to keep the weight off?" I would tell people that it was my diet and intermittent fasting, when in all reality I had to reduce my food intake to one meal per day, that's all I could afford. I was rail thin, the skinniest I had ever been. Before this time I was athletic, well put together, I was proud of my physique. Now it was a mere function of I just didn't have the money. I was too embarrassed to admit what was going on. I had to keep this façade up that everything was okay, but it wasn't.

There were a few times that my power was shut off, for a few days at a time even. I just didn't have it. My bank account was in a constant state of overdraft, and the fees took a toll on any chance of getting ahead. I hated asking for help, so I didn't.

With what money I had, I would buy ice and put whatever groceries I had, mostly condiments looking back in a cooler in my garage. I would charge my phone by sitting in the car parked in the garage as well. I certainly didn't want my neighbors to notice, like why is Justin sitting in his car in the driveway for hours at a time. I couldn't accept assistance like food stamps without having to report it to my compliance office at work on our annual meeting questionnaires. Even if I could, I wouldn't have. I could've attended a food bank. But in my head I couldn't get over the sense of pride I had. Even though I was in incredible need, I could never accept myself in that position. I know this situation perpetuated my mental illness in many ways. I was losing my confidence. Whatever shred of pride I held onto just wouldn't let me accept that sort of charity. So I learned to accept going without. All while this was going on, I always paid my child support. That was paid first. I should have been evicted many times over, but my landlord was incredibly understanding of my situation and would often give me an extension for being late. There was no water coming from my rock, that fucker was dried out.

After taking every means possible in reducing any expenditures I had control over, I knew I needed to do something to bring more money to the table. I had sold every last possession I had that was worth anything. eBay, Craigslist, Offer Up, Facebook marketplace, I used just about every platform out there to hawk whatever I had left. The only thing I kept, as they were my prized possession, were my Candlestick Park seats. When the stadium was torn down to build condos, and the 49ers moved to Santa Clara, the seats were being sold by the pair. I had grown up going to Candlestick park with my family to watch Giants games and 49ers games live, and it was to me an incredible piece of nostalgia. They made me remember who I was before I started my nosedive. They gave me hope that one day I could sit in those again as the man I was before. I told myself that I'd be buried in those before I would sell them off.

When I ran out of possessions to sell, I knew I had to get another job. I was already working at the bank during the day, so the only time I had was at night. My mental state at that time was fragile. It was difficult for me to do my job successfully. I had lost a lot of my confidence. I had a hard time looking people in the eye, not because I was being dishonest or unethical. It was I was so embarrassed and ashamed of how I let myself get to that point, I had a hard time looking at myself in the mirror let alone someone else. This took a toll on my productivity as a result. I was in this cycle where I needed to make more money to quell the stress, but the stress made it almost impossible to make more money and be successful in that role. I was floundering, but I still had a good rapport with my colleagues and management, who I kept from knowing there was any inclination of me having a hardship.

I used to donate plasma at a local blood bank in the shitty part of town. I actually would frequent two places. One would give you a prepaid debit card that didn't have any cash value, but you could purchase items at the store with. The other gave you a card that you kept, and they'd load money onto it, but it still only allowed for point-of-sale transactions.

These places were so sad. Everyone was welcome, and when I say everyone that's what I mean. This place attracted anyone that was willing to do whatever they could to feed there families and to stay upright. There were honest hard-working people that used this as a means to supplement the shortfalls they were facing with other employment, and I had felt a sense of community with them. They were going through the same issues I was and the money was going to the right causes.

Then there were the other folks. These were the people that used this as an opportunity to pay for drugs, and they often would come in high as fuck on whatever they were on. There were sometimes fights in line. Imagine this lobby you would walk into and facing the front desk where you would be admitted, there was this huge line snaking up and down. This line was always full of people waiting, a lot like the kinds of lines you'd see at the DMV. People were tense as fuck. Either they were simply tired of waiting for as long as they were, or you had people strung out on god knows what. There'd be people going through withdrawals and the only way for them to get their fix was to wait this line, donate their plasma, and likely trade the proceeds for drugs just thereafter. People would try to cut the line, or they would see a friend in line and cut in with them that way. These places were always a shit show, and the crazy thing is, they were taking plasma straight from people that had just gotten strung out in the parking lot prior to.

This was fucking amazing, and as frustrating and embarrassing it was for me to be there, It really gave me perspective as to what these people were going through. It was awkward when you'd be standing in line and all of a sudden a guy nods off from being on dope and you were his landing zone. As uncomfortable it made me, it was my necessary evil. It put food in my belly and gas in my tank when I wouldn't have otherwise. The people watching was entertaining though.

Once you were admitted you would go into this large room filled with medical beds where the back was tilted upward so you would sit at an angle. It was always freezing cold in there, and the cold only got worse when it was your time to donate. The nurse would come by and swab your arms. They then would put a needle in each forearm, each hooked to a tube. Both tubes connected to a machine that would then collect your blood and separate the plasma which would collect into a bag. The best description I could give you of what Plasma looked like to me was dehydrated urine. It had this dark yellow opaque tint to it. As I understood it, the needle in the other forearm was inserting whatever remained as a byproduct from extracting the plasma into the bag. This process usually took an hour for me, but just depended on how long it took to fill the bag.

The place in the shitty strip mall in South Sacramento you would donate one bag per visit, and you had to wait a few days until you could come back. They'd give you a cookie and juice box to get your blood sugar back up so you didn't faint when you stood back up. They'd then give you a gift card and send you on your merry way. I stopped going to this place because they would give you a much larger amount per your first few donations to get you excited about coming back. But after a while they would end up giving you much less, until I finally gave up.

The other place I went to was out in the foothills of Sacramento County in this nice office complex filled with various doctors' offices. Though the clientele was similar to those in South Sacramento, there weren't as many beds so it wasn't the shit show of people watching I had grown accustomed to. This place was much cleaner, the nurses were much friendlier, and it didn't have as much of a demeaning vibe to it as the other had. Here though, you would sign up for a timed session, typically 2-3 hours long. They would hook you up to the same types of machines, but here you had your own room and your own personal TV you could stream shows and movies on. This made the experience that much more comfortable, but being there for that long with needles hooked up to both arms it would certainly try your patience. I had a hard time not bending my arms, especially when I had to itch my face or something. When you did, the machine would start blaring bells and whistles until the nurse had to come in and make sure everything was still intact.

Here they would give you more money because you were there for like a half a day, and you ended up donating a lot more than just one bag at a time. The other place would end up giving you like $30 per donation, this was longer and they'd give you like $50-$75 per donation because you were giving so much more.

Was it worth it? At the time yeah. Though demeaning and embarrassing, it was still honest. It was engrained in me at such an early age in life by my parents that stealing was something so wrong. Thus that was never going to be an option for me, ever. I remember vividly growing up, I was maybe 5 or 6 years old and I had eaten a piece of candy from those self-serve bins that they had at the grocery store. My mom made me go up to the manager and apologize, I was crying profusely. That experience never left me, and it would prove to be a foundation for my moral and ethical compass for everything I would do thereafter. When buying groceries at Wal-Mart, I always went through the self-checkout lines. On a few occasions I'd be there ringing up my items, and in the corner of my eye I'd see others doing the same. However they wouldn't pay. They would ring everything up, bag it, and walk on out like they already had. This was so frustrating for me, as being the honest person I am, I'd struggle to pay for the items I could afford – but I always paid. Then you'd have these degenerates just walk out with a cart full of groceries without paying a dime. Hey Wal-Mart, your shareholders would be a lot happier if your loss prevention team actually prevented loss!

There was one way that I made extra money that felt incredibly violating, and that was donating bone marrow. I have done it twice. I thought I had learned my lesson the first time I did it, but I needed the money so I did it again maybe 6 months later. For this donation they'd give you a gift card for $250. Fuck I wish there was a way I could have circumvented doing that, but the same place I was donating plasma to was offering the service, so it was hard to pass up.

They would always praise you for your donating, saying that it goes toward saving lives and groundbreaking research, but they weren't the ones with a fucking drill in their back! This whole process took about an hour to complete, maybe less, but it was so much more painful. They would lay you down on a hospital bed face down. They would pull your shirt up and your underwear down to about half ass cheek. They would clean the area at the small of your back, your tailbone really, with an iodine substance. You would get a few numbing shots, and those needles hurt like fuck. Once you were numb enough they brought the drill in. A drill. A fucking drill! The same type of cordless drill you'd buy at Home Depot to drill holes in your wall to hang family pictures with. That drill!

At this point my mind was racing, and I immediately regretted what I had signed up to do, but it was too late. They go on to tell me that they would drill two holes into the small of my back, one at a time, and that they'd then use a syringe to extract the marrow from within my bones. That's exactly what they did. I don't know what made me most uncomfortable, the drilling or the suctioning. The drilling made a vibration as the drill bit spun around digging into the bone. They would exude pressure forcing it down like you were having a hard time drilling through wood and the only thing that would allow you to drill further was to put more pressure on it. At this point I'd hear the drill whirling around just a few feet from my face. You could hear the drill as it was grinding away at your bones. You could see what looked like smoke coming from the drill. I could only imagine that it was the powdered bone particles that billowed in the air, similar to that of saw dust when working with wood. The smell of the burning bone as a result of the heat the drill created was one I can never forget. Then the drill would reach its climax when it had penetrated through the bone. They would then take a syringe and draw this thick bone marrow liquid out of the hole they had just drilled. I was numb this whole time, so it wasn't so much the pain I was experiencing it was the discomfort. The suctioning was an equally violating experience, a feeling that I had never experienced before. Just when you thought it was over, they'd do the entire process all over again on the other side of my back. I did this on two separate occasions. Just recounting the experience makes me want to vomit. How I could ever put myself in the position to have to do this, it's hard to come to grips with, but I did.

I had so many hands in my cookie jar, there was nothing left. Often I would get paid, and three days later after paying all of my bills I wouldn't have anything left to feed myself until the next payday rolled around. This was a necessary evil, and despite going to a good cause, it felt evil. I felt violated. Was this good for my mental psyche, nope! I knew that I needed another way to generate additional income. I had to get a second job. It had to be flexible enough that I could do at night and on the weekends I didn't have my kids. I had no experience bartending, so that wasn't an option. I wasn't tough enough to be a bouncer at the door, so no dice there. The only other option I could think of was rideshare. I had an economical vehicle and I enjoyed driving, so it was the most natural fit. However, just like many other times in my life this would bring all new types of experiences, some so crazy you couldn't make this kind of stuff up. Needless to say, I was along for the ride. I never would have thought the company would put me through what I ultimately experienced. Like the story of David vs. Goliath, I would be faced with the task of taking them to court over what was so evidently the difference between right and wrong. To the fuckers' dismay – I won too.

CHAPTER VI.
RIDESHARE: DAVID VS. GOLIATH

Don't forget to tip your driver. The kind of bullshit rideshare drivers are put through by some of their passengers, when all they're trying to do is earn a living, can be downright despicable. These are people just like you and me. Whether these are the full-time grinders, or those needing to supplement their 9-5's, they need to be treated with respect. You see the all too many BuzzFeed dashcam videos of people getting out of hand, whether its verbal abuse and even sometimes turning physical. Now 9 out of 10 passengers typically behaved themselves, which makes the job palatable, but the other 1 of 10 you really don't know what you're going to get. People forget that just because you paid for something doesn't give you carte blanche ability to mistreat them however you like.

On and off for over 2 years I was one of them. I relied heavily on the supplementary income it provided me when I was also working full-time, and even way more so when I quit the bank I was working for. For me I liked the freedom. The flexibility was paramount, and this is why I think it is so attractive to others as well. If you had a reliable car, a clean-enough driving record, and no felonies it gave you the ability to earn on your time not someone else's. Every ride was different. There was a bit of a thrill of the unknown. You didn't really know who you were going to be picking up. Until they got in your car you really wouldn't know where you were headed, with the exception of any rides over 45 minutes in duration, you would get notified in case you didn't want to drive that far. For the most part that was the fun of it. Some people preferred to work the daytime and the morning commute. Some preferred working nights and weekends. Pick-ups and drop-offs for events always provided a high demand, and in many cases the driver would be paid a premium based on the supply and demand of drivers at the venue at that time.

I drove them all. I was in such desperate need for income, that these platforms really allowed me to hustle at my own pace. I was a hustler. Not the kind of hustler that drove way too fast and frantic that would likely end up in a bad rating and complaint. Not the kind of hustler that was shiesty, or the type that would always give you some sob story to try and generate a higher tip. My hustle was that I am going to provide the best service I could possible, always being active, and determined to hit my numbers every time I was out there. Based on how many hours I was planning on working, I would put an income goal in for the night. If I exceeded that goal, I wouldn't' stop until the time I had allotted was complete. If I didn't meet that goal, then I usually kept working until I did.

I lived in Sacramento, which at the time I was driving wasn't providing high enough demand to justify the time spent. I tried it locally, and most often you would have to drive quite the distance to pick someone up because maybe you were the closest driver, but still far away. Once you picked up your passenger, you didn't have any control over where they were going. You could drive 15-20 minutes somewhere, and end up driving them just 5 minutes away. The income sucked, and on top of that I still had too much pride to be recognized by someone I knew locally. Rideshare driving was a godsend for me, and other people that needed to earn income. But it was an incredibly humbling experience. I went from a Regional Vice President making a six-figure salary to taking lip from some teenager over a $6 ride. Those factors, I didn't want to see anyone I knew locally and that the money was so bad I decided to drive in the San Francisco Bay Area instead.

Bay Area rideshare demand was high. I was always getting requests, and I never had to drive super far away to get there either. Using serving tables as an analogy, if my car was the table, driving in the bay area gave me the ability to turn my tables much quicker. My goal was to always have someone in my car. If no one was in my car, I wasn't getting paid. Bay Area driving isn't everyone's cup of tea, but I was comfortable with it. I grew up there, so I was still familiar in my surroundings. A lot of drivers that lived in Sacramento would do the same, because it made the most sense.

95% of the time you wouldn't get a ride on your way driving the 80 or so miles west. Even if you were 'dead-heading' on your hour and a half drive there, the action you would have access to for me justified it. If I planned on working 9-12 hours, even with the 3 hours there and back when I was alone, I still would make more than I would driving those same hours in Sacramento. As far as shifts, I worked them all. Days, Mornings, Nights, Weekends, Holidays, I did it. I worked them all especially when I was working it full-time. Concerts and Warriors games were my favorite. Concerts almost always provided a longer trip, and due to high demand for drivers when they had let out, a lot of the times based on supply and demand the premium for the ride would get pretty lofty.

At the time I had a way of working the system. I would accept a ride, and if it wasn't a far enough drive, I'd cancel and accept a new ride until I got the one I wanted. If you did this too many times consecutively they'd kick you off the platform, but I always managed to have good luck. The best ride I had from a concert was when I worked Bottle Rock in Napa one year. Bottle Rock is this badass 3-day event in downtown Napa that would attract acts of all kinds even some of the biggest. I'd liken it to a Stagecoach, Lalapalooza, or Coachella.

The reason why it was so lucrative for rideshare drivers is that Napa was not built logistically to provide transportation to that many people in such a small space. When I arrived it was a mass exodus of people. Many had been out in the sun all day, were exhausted and just wanted to go home. If a group had gone together, maybe they would split the high cost of the ride home. For others, they just had to bite the bullet per se, as there was no real alternative unless you'd wait out the demand which could've taken hours. Did I feel bad when I had accepted a ride from Napa to San Francisco that would pay me $350? Maybe a little, but if someone was going to receive it, why not me right?

Warriors games were always good rides as they played in West Oakland at the time, and unless you were taking them to an alternate transit means, like the BART rail system, usually you were taking a fan home at a distance that was lucrative. If I was lucky they were cool and wanted to talk about the game, where I'd get to feel kind of like I was living vicariously through them. My favorite ride was working in Santa Clara during the week, a pretty routine trip, but it was a 49ers player going to practice. He wasn't a big name at the time, and was even just on the practice squad, but I knew him. He would turn out to be a very productive player for the 49ers in years to come, and even aided my fantasy football team a time or two.

Those experiences made the job fun. Was it stressful, at times yes, but nowhere near the levels of stress I would experience trying to find alternate means of income.

With thousands of rides to my credit, I certainly had my share of war stories. I've had my ride thrown-up in twice. The first I luckily had a trash bag under my seat, and was able to get it to them in time. It was a husband and wife that may have been retired, whom I had picked up from (SFO) San Francisco International Airport and ended taking them out to the East Bay for a ride that took about 45 minutes. This was the typical story of old people using Apps they had no idea what they were doing, and to their credit they were just trying to select the cheapest option. What they didn't realize was that they had selected a carpool or shared ride with someone else. I hated these rides because the interactions between the random passengers were almost always super awkward. In this case they had no idea, and even got mad at me for picking up the other young passenger at the next gate before venturing off. I was to drop the younger gal off in the City before I was to take the older couple across the bay to their destination. By the way if you're a Bay Area local, you don't call San Francisco by it's namesake, it's the City. It's not San Fran, or the dreaded Frisco – which I'm sure is an awesome place in Texas, but certainly not a locally acceptable nickname for the city by the bay.

I also hated these pooled rides especially from the airport, as with the influx of bags, a lot of the times the overflow was the front seat. I had a Prius for a while, and then switched to a Ford Fusion Energi, which allowed me access to the diamond HOV lane based on my plug-in hybrid stickers. The Prius was small. The Fusion was roomier, but whoever designed this thing didn't have trunk space in mind, as that was where the hybrid battery was housed, and you couldn't fit more than one big suitcase or two smaller one's if you were lucky.

So on this trip we're on the freeway about to get off the exit. I had the extra suitcases in my front seat, so there was the younger gal smashed up against two larger human beings, and now this guy was getting sick. I'm like fuck dude, please don't puke in my car, and certainly don't puke on this poor girl. I was able to get him the trash bag in the nick of time so he wouldn't blow chunks all over. In my rear view mirror I could see the gal just cringe at the sound of what was happening. I truly felt bad, however she was the one that wanted to save a buck by not taking her own ride, so in that circumstance those are the risks you take. I dropped her off, and apologized as much as I could for her experience, despite having nothing to do with the guy getting sick. He ended up heaving almost the whole way home, and it was super awkward, but those are the risks that I was taking in my role as their driver.

The other time someone got sick in my car, it got everywhere. It was unannounced, gave me no forewarning and smelled god awful. I had picked up this gal from a nice restaurant hotel in the Embarcadero district of the City, and was to drop her off about

20 minutes away to the Excelsior district. I picked her up and greeted her as she entered the back seat. She was well dressed and looked like she was on her way home from a nice dinner out with friends. I was never much of a talker when driving. I hated being a passenger with an oversharing driver that wanted to share their life story, so I was considerate. I would always gauge if they wanted to talk, and was open to conversing if they were but never pressed it.

I confirmed our destination and asked her how her evening was, and her response was a rude and curt "I just want to get home as soon as possible." This was not your typical response when asking how people are doing, but I just took it as she didn't want to chat and wanted to go home. What I would soon find out was that wasn't the case at all, she wanted to get home as soon as possible because she was about to get sick and wouldn't make it home in time. So we're driving on Hwy 280, not exactly a highway conducive to pulling over as there were a lot of skyways with no shoulder access. Mind you at the time I thought she was just being a little rude, not anticipating that she'd projectile vomit all over the back of the front seat, onto herself, and all over her feet at the floorboard.

Oh god this was a disgusting mess. I couldn't pull over. It smelled so bad I had to roll the windows down. From what I could tell it was seafood and chardonnay. She said it was cold and asked me to roll the window up, I certainly wasn't going to acquiesce, as the smell now made me feel like I was going to puke as well. I got her home despite the minutes feeling like hours. I think she felt bad, but she was in such disarray that she must not have been thinking all that clearly. When she left she dropped a $20 bill on the floor for me, as like a tip. Under normal circumstances that would've been a very nice tip, but not for someone that just violated my vehicle. On top of that the bill landed directly in the vomit. I gladly took it, cleaned it off, and even used it to buy more cleaning supplies at the Walgreens up the street.

When passengers get sick in your car, the rideshare platform will pay for the car to get detailed, I think it was like $100 maybe. But this happened at night, at the beginning of my shift nonetheless. I needed that car cleaned to hit my daily nut, I couldn't wait until morning to get it professionally cleaned, so I did it myself. It took a shit ton of paper towels and Pine-sol spray, and because she tried to puke out the window when it was clearly closed I spent like an hour cleaning it with Windex. Why did it take so long? Well as soon as it was clean, I'd roll the window down, and it would come up with streaks of vomit. Only until after numerous times of that same process I was able to get it clean enough to continue my night. So yeah lady, thank you for the $20 tip, but I still sent pictures of the mess you made and collected my $100. These are the things drivers have to put up with, so even if you're the nicest most courteous passenger, they're not all like you.

I never got into any physical confrontation with my passengers, as no one really put me in a position where I felt I had to. At the time I wasn't a big guy, but I was 6' tall and 220 lbs. I was pretty lean as I would go hours without eating. I have tattoos, which were pretty evident if I was wearing t-shirt as I normally did. I never acted tough, but I didn't give anyone the impression I was a pushover either. The only time things almost got physical was during Fleet Week. This was a week in the late summer in the City, when Navy ships would line up along the piers up from Golden Gate Park to China Basin. There were always a ton of uniformed cadets excited to explore the various landmarks and attractions. It was certainly a great week for business with the influx of people. On the weekend is when it got really busy because they had a spectacular air show. I always enjoyed the Tom Cats and Blue Angels, whose aerial stunts defied the laws of gravity as spectators watched in awe. During the week they would practice. If you happened to be driving in the Financial District at the time of their practices the sounds of these jets would bounce and reverberate off of the tall buildings often so loud setting off car alarms as they passed.

For the most part the air show was an excuse to get hammered with your friends and party. The influx of people needing rides as a result made demand quite high, and certainly a good day for business. That day was the closest I ever got to being physical with someone, as their behavior was insulting, and at the time I had no patience for it. I picked up this group of 4, 2 girls and 2 guys, from an apartment in the Marina. The Marina is a beautiful area of the city right along the bay. The homes were affluent and all had personally distinctive architecture some from even a century ago. It was not a cheap place to live, and the group that I picked up exuded this snobby sense of entitlement that wouldn't end up going over in their favor.

I pick them up and they're hammered, which was to be expected because that was the mantra of the day, and I certainly wasn't one that wanted to kill their vibe. But they get in and slam the doors. They had to be in their very early twenties. There were two girls and another guy in the back seat, and the other guy sat up front. We departed and were on our way to the destination, which wasn't more than 10-15 minutes away. The guy up front though, he was playing on his phone and hadn't put his seatbelt on. I didn't really give a shit if he had it on or not, even from a safety perspective, it would've been his nose to my dashboard. But it was the fact that the constant beeping was going off repeatedly, it was annoying as fuck. I finally stopped the car until he did in fact buckle his seatbelt, but not without giving me attitude in doing so. Then as we were driving the guy in the backseat starts hooking up with one of the girls next to him. I'm not a prude, but have some decency to not do that in my back seat. Their hands all over each other, as he was feeling her up and she was feeling him down. I could hear them making out, the smacking of their lips was like a meat grinder next to my ears. Finally I got so uncomfortable and fed up that I asked them to stop. I said something like, "Is this something you do in all of your rides?" in disgust. Their reaction was like a roll of their eyes with a response of, just drive dude. At this point I had had enough. I was hella nice, until you took my kindness for weakness, then I was going to throw you out. I quickly pulled over, I ended the ride on my phone, gave the passenger a 1-star rating, and said the rides over "It's time to get the fuck out." Then the douche up front tried to argue with me to keep going. I looked him dead in the eye, and started to say "If I have to get out of this car..." As soon as he heard that he knew it was time to get out.

I was so angry. I drive that car with my babies in the backseat when I'm not ridesharing to earn a living. I felt so offended. I was so appalled at them for getting mad at me for calling them out on their behavior, like it was my fault. God the sense of entitlement of some of the yuppies I had to drive in the City during those years really stretched the level of humility I was willing to accept. Luckily that day I didn't get out of the car, because as they say, assault is a crime and I would've seen the worst of it in the end.

One shift I happened to receive a ride request at like 3:30 am from a sketchy part of the Tenderloin. This was the skid row of the City where homeless addicts, drug dealers, pimps and prostitutes were ever-present. This was a part of town that was dangerous for you to be in during the daytime let alone in the dead of night. I had seen it all. It was an open-air drug market. It was not uncommon to be at a stoplight and there be an addict nodded off with a needle in their arm just feet away from your car door. It would not be uncommon to see people taking shits on the sidewalk. I've seen fights. The most powerless I felt was sitting in traffic near Columbus and Broadway when I witnessed this woman get attacked by another woman stealing her purse and cell phone. By the time I noticed and could jump out of the car to save the day, the lady had already took off. The crime in the City seemed to get progressively worse and worse. As long as you had the mass populous of people giving handouts supporting the addicts' drug habits, you'd have drug dealers and the crime that came with it. For those that have seen the culture of the City shift this way throughout the decades is so disheartening. This beautiful City by the Bay had turned into the dirtiest and one of the least-safe places to visit. The unsuspecting tourists were prime targets, and I think that Is what I had witnessed when the girl had been attacked.

Those memories you just can't forget.

So when I had received the request so late at night in such a shotty area of the City, I was incredibly reluctant. I pulled over at the address I was requested, and of course the street was full of shady characters looking me up and down. I locked my doors and gave myself just a minute for this guy to arrive or I was out of there. Why didn't I just cancel and leave? I needed the money, and at the same time there was this curiosity I had. I had definitely driven some shady characters during my time. I've driven hookers, drug dealers, and guys I could only describe as pimps though I never knew for sure. My mantra was don't fuck with me or my car and everything will be alright. Was I in a position to fight off someone in my backseat with a knife to my throat or gun to my back, nope – but that was the risk I was taking.

So finally as all of my spidey senses are on high alert and looking in one direction I hear a knock on the other window, and there he was. I always confirmed their name with what was on the app, and sure enough it was him. Nowadays I see when I request rides, most drivers have their front seat pulled all the way forward circumventing anyone from sitting in the front seat next to them. That was a fantastic tactic that I just didn't have the foresight to employ at the time unfortunately. So this guy hops in the front seat. He's an older gentleman in maybe his 50's. His wardrobe looked straight out of the 1970's. He had a tan mid-length leather jacket, the kind that you could tie at the waist. His matching tan leather hat was one like a baseball cap but the cap portion ballooned out like a mushroom. Pardon my description but he looked like he came straight from the movie Shaft central casting. I wasn't one to judge or discriminate, but that's what I remember. He said that he needed to go out to the Dog Patch area but really

we ended up in another shady part of town further down 3rd Street called Bayview / Hunter's Point. This for many drivers may have set off a red flag, and I could totally see people rejecting the ride because they didn't feel safe going there, but I was kind of intrigued. I thought to myself, "Ooh what kind of shit are we going to get into tonight."

He was very chill and relaxed during the drive. He was preoccupied texting someone on his phone, so there wasn't any awkward silence where I would have to spark up conversation. When we arrived at the destination he politely asked if I could stay there for a few minutes as he'd be right back and needed a ride back from where I had picked him up from. Roundtrip ride requests were not uncommon, and since it was so late that I probably wouldn't get another ride right away, I obliged. This gave me an opportunity to check my phone, see what kind of messages I had, get the scores from the games the night before.

Not more than a few moments later, as soon as I started checking my phone, he comes back to the door in a hurried panic like he had lost something. He was looking all around the front seat, underneath, at the doorsill and console feverishly, like he had lost something very valuable to him. He kept asking me, "Did you take it? Did you take it?" I responded back like, "What the fuck dude, I didn't take anything." He'd continue to check and then would pat down his pockets and check all of those ultimately letting out this huge sigh of relief like he had found what he had thought he had lost was with him the entire time. He subtly apologized then closed the door. All the while I'm taking stock of what had just happened. Normal people would have gotten the fuck out of there. But I'm not normal, so I stuck around for him. He came back, sat down, and acted just as chill and relaxed as he was when I picked him up. I dropped him off back at the corner I had picked him up from without incident. Was it a drug buy, very likely. I'm not the sharpest tool in the shed, but I have a pretty strong street sense, so that's what I think had happened. Could it have ended a whole lot worse for me, absolutely. Did I stick around for the sheer fact that I thought this was an awesome story and I wanted to see it play out – you fucking know it!

Despite all of the precarious situations I'd find myself in, and the enjoyment therein, after a few years I did start to burn out. By that time I knew how to play the system. I would work for twelve hours on one platform until they kicked you off for a mandatory rest period. Then I would hop on the other. There were shifts that I ended up driving for over 24 hours. That was the commitment of my hustle. It would turn out to be the reason I had to stop not that long later. I had such a strong work ethic, and need to care for my kids, I was willing to work as many hours as they'd let me. Was it safe? No, of course not. There's only so much coffee and red bull you can drink to keep yourself as alert as you needed to be to drive safely. I think I pulled it off well enough to where I don't think people noticed. If they did, I never heard of it.

The 'come to Jesus' moment for me was when I got into an accident. Thank god It wasn't any worse than it was, because it certainly could have been. It was completely my fault. I was on one of my 24 hour driving benders. It happened mid-day out by the San Jose airport on a busy thoroughfare with freeway access to Hwy 101. I was in the fast lane and wasn't speeding, but as I went through an intersection for the briefest of moment I nodded off. As I went through the intersection I had clipped the median separating my lane from a turn lane in the opposite direction. My wheel went up on the curb and I hit a wood No U-turn sign that ended up slamming up against the side of this lady's Mercedes knocking her side mirror off and scraping the driver's side of the car. I immediately came to, but it was too late. The damage to my car was much worse. I ended up popping 3 of my tires, bending the rims as I inched my way over to the closest parking lot.

I ended up having to spend my weeks' worth of earnings to buy new spare wheels and tires just to make it home. It was a very sobering drive home, and I think that's when I realized I needed a change. What is the definition of insanity? Doing the same thing over and over again, and expecting a different result – right? I was most certainly insane from that perspective. I was lucky enough to drive home that night. Luckily it didn't happen when I had a passenger with me. I could've seriously hurt myself, and even worse seriously hurt someone else.

This experience made me realize that driving for as long as I was, didn't get me to where I needed to be in life. Like many other circumstances in my life, this was the band aid when I really needed stitches. It was a perpetual cycle, and based on the course I was set, It wasn't going to end well.

Somehow I was able to take a few weeks off to look for something full-time in my field of study, something that didn't require the stress and rigors of what I was doing before, and ultimately I was able to land a new job at a smaller credit union back home.

Before I did finally secure better employment, I still had to drive to earn an income. Since I had a choice, I made the decision to drive exclusively at night instead of during the day, and especially not during both. Nighttime driving was a lot easier than having to deal with the influx of cars clogging the congested roadways of the Bay Area during the day.

I typically drove from 10:00 pm to 10:00 am. The roadways remained pretty calm until about 6:00 am, and at that time I was only in the thick of it for a few hours until the morning commute concluded and I made my way back to Sacramento. For the first part of my shift I spent most of my time taking people home from dinners and bars, as well as those working in the service industry. I'd make pick-ups pretty consistently no matter what day it was from 10:00 pm until things always slowed down between 3:00 am and 5:00 am. This is where I was king of the value menu, taking my fast food breaks at whatever was open at the time. If fast food wasn't an option I could usually find a Denny's or a Mel's Diner to post up at until business picked back up. Then the remainder of my morning was spent taking people to work. The produce packing district workers in the City were often my first rides thereafter as they had to arrive for work in the wee hours of the morning. If not them, a lot of airport rides. Once 7:00 am rolled around it was a mixture of all types of rides wherever the morning commute would take me.

I had driven at night so many times, one rideshare platform sent me a virtual trophy for completing over 500 5-star nighttime rides. It was something I was more than comfortable with. Surprisingly for me the night crowd seemed nicer than the daytime folks. But that comfort certainly took a turn one night in mid-November 2018, and this would drastically change my mindset and comfort level with not necessarily the interaction with the passengers, but the actual rideshare platform itself.

My attitude towards ridesharing took a pretty drastic turn on November 14th 2018. In the wee hours of that Wednesday @ 12:11 am I was dispatched to a ride request in Newark, Ca maybe 20 minutes south of Oakland. The fare destination requested through the app was to Monterey Park, CA approximately 366 miles away in Los Angeles County. This was my second ride of my 10-hour shift, and felt no reluctance in accepting the request as I was prepared to drive that duration already. I figured I would make the same amount of money, for possibly less driving that same timeframe around the Bay Area, so I saw it as a great opportunity to earn while only putting freeway miles on my vehicle.

The passengers did not speak English very well, which wasn't the slightest bit of a red flag, as I am anything but a racist and would drive people of all backgrounds, colors, sexual orientations, etc. Their Trip Detail included verbiage in their native language, which was unusual, but regardless I abided by the rideshare's zero tolerance policy for discrimination against passengers. The trip in total was 5 hours and 3 minutes.

As I'm on my way back up north, driving the 350+ miles back home, I got a message from the app that would make my heart sink. Shortly following the completion of the ride request I was notified by the platform that the fare of $421.17 was adjusted to $0.00! I was completely flabbergasted. Their explanation was due to: "Rider Fraud. This fare was adjusted following a report that this charge was not authorized by the payment account owner. As a result, we are not able to process this fare."

What the fuck right??!! Throughout the duration of my drive

back to Northern California I had corresponded with their Driver Support Team and was notified that an inquiry into the trip was taking place. I thought surely this was a mistake. No way could they be denying me payment of this ride for the reasons they had laid out. I figured this would get hashed out and I'd be paid within a few days at most.

The following day November 15 2018 I had received notice from their Support Team. In response they stated "We've reviewed the details of this trip and our records indicate that this was an unauthorized trip." Whatever the fuck that meant.

They'd continue with, "Examples of unauthorized trips include: deliberately increasing the time or distance of a trip, accepting trips without the intention to complete, including provoking riders to cancel, creating dummy rider or driver accounts for fraudulent purposes, and intentionally accepting or completing fraudulent, or falsified trips." Also, I was suggested: "Going forward, please only use the partner app to accept and complete trips on authorized rides", and subsequently denied payment of the fare.

So basically they were throwing around accusations that could not be any farther from the truth. I never deliberately increased the time of the trip, if anything I made the trip that much more efficient. The speed limit on Interstate 5 in the middle of nowhere is 70 mph, but no one goes 70 miles per hour unless you're a big rig. So I certainly wasn't increasing the time or distance of the trip. I definitely didn't accept a ride without the intention to complete. What am I going to do cut their ride short and drop them off in Los Banos?! Sure didn't! I never provoked a rider to cancel – we drove the entire 350+ miles. Their last accusation I had never even heard of prior to this, and that was creating dummy driver or rider accounts for fraudulent purposes – but I'm pretty sure that's what they did to me. Accusing me of accepting or completing fraudulent trips on authorized rides?!? I was clearly just using their shitty platform. I didn't know these people, and I certainly wasn't in collusion with them to get them a free ride to Southern

California.

In essence I was duped by the riders, but I didn't know until the app told me so. Since when is checking passengers' credit card information to see if it was valid a responsibility of the driver? It never was and couldn't be, I had no way to tell either way. Simply said, they request the ride, I pick them up, and I provide safe passage to their desired destination. If anything it was the rideshare app's responsibility, not mine. I was pissed, not only because I was out over $400. That stung, but not as much as the accusation that I am a liar, cheat, and fraud. Fuck them, I'm the most honest person out there. Passengers would forget stuff in the backseat all the time, and I always went out of my way to get it back to them. This all for no reason other than it was the right thing to do. At this point they had lost all respect I had for them. I used to think they were the best, giving people like myself an alternate means to generate income, with the flexibility to do so on our time. Turns out they were going to blame the little guy for their failures in safeguarding this from happening. It's a fucking tech company, should they have the wherewithal to circumvent that from happening in the first place?!? Maybe if they did, I would have dropped their punk-asses off in the middle of nowhere!

I was personally insulted. In my 2 years as an driver on this particular platform, I had accumulated 1,252 Trips with a 4.93/5.00 rating. I had accumulated over 500 5-star trips, and as I was accustomed to driving the early hours of the morning – I had achieved over 100 late night 5-Star trips as well. The Late-night trips were a necessary means to support my family in holding two full-time jobs at times.

Just weeks before Christmas, the earnings from this fare were earmarked for gifts for my two young children. I was appalled and outraged by the accusation that I acted fraudulently in any capacity in reference to my time with said rideshare. I was ready to sue those motherfuckers, as anyone in my position would have had every right to do so, or at least you'd think I'd be able to. I spent a day walking around the City, speaking with those at the county court office as well as those at the Federal level. With all of my research I wasn't finding what I was looking for. I wanted to get my piece of justice out of these scumbags in any way I could. I could blast them on internet review boards, but that would never amount to anything other than a further souring of the taste in my mouth.

Finally I was able to find what I was looking for, kind of. I googled "how to sue (insert name of rideshare)?" The result was not what I had expected, because based on what I was reading I couldn't. I had to go through an arbitration service, one that they had pre-selected nonetheless. So once I found out this was the only course of action in getting paid what was rightfully mine, I decided to dive in head first.

The first thing I needed to do was file a claim, so I wrote the most eloquent and articulate response to their allegations and submitted to the group that would ultimately hear my case. I wrote that based on the evidence that I have provided, how can they even substantiate such a claim? It is their responsibility to ensure that the Rider can provide valid payment at the time of the ride – not the Driver's! If the fare was purchased via a fraudulent method of payment – why am I still directed via the Driver App to pick up said passengers!? I asserted that putting any burden on the Driver's discretion would be in violation of their Anti-Discrimination Policy.

I accepted a ride request through the Authorized rideshare Driver's App. I drove the passengers to their desired destination that they requested within the app. Upon completion of my trip, I was denied wages. Furthermore, I was accused of being in collusion with a Rider using a fraudulent credit card – which was completely false. To deny a Driver wages and accuse them of fraud – and still allow the Driver continued access to the Driver app – just didn't make sense. If I had committed such a crime, wouldn't they boot me off of their platform? But no they allowed me to continue to work. This being something I was so incredibly reluctant to do, however I had kids to feed, so I had to place all animosity I had for them aside.

If anything they should be held liable for their defamatory policy and subsequent fraud-related procedures. My monetary claim included my plea for punitive damages, as well as any costs incurred by the trip itself, and subsequent efforts during the duration of arbitration. This was a process that went on for 12 months, and I had to pester the arbitration firm to press harder throughout, as they would not proceed until they got paid by the rideshare platform. Of course they are going to delay the process as long as they can, they knew they were wrong. So they made us wait until they absolutely had to pay the arbitrator to hear my case.

I had asked for punitive damages, pain and suffering I called it. In any other circumstance if you were denied wages on services rendered by your employer, you damn sure would have the right to do so. But not them. These sleazebags had written into the fine print of the driver's employment agreement, The Transportation Service Agreement (TSA), that if found at fault all I could recover were my lost wages. Way to bury that into the fine print of our contracts without us really knowing what it prevailed them the ability to do to us!

Ultimately I would be denied any punitive damages, but there was a chance I would get paid what they had owed me. Once it came down to finally meeting, knowing what I did about their TSA precluding me of the ability to be rewarded additional funds, I decided to make it as difficult for them as possible. They requested we meet with the arbitrator via phone or video conference, which I denied. I made them drive their happy asses out to Sacramento so I could look at them in the eyes. For me it was incredibly personal, and for them I was just a box they needed to check off and move on their merry way. I wasn't going to allow them the satisfaction of getting off that easy. They were wrong, and I was going to prove it. If they tried any way to put this back on me, I would dance all over them.

I loved the Arbitrator, he was gangster. This attorney was semi-retired with decades of experience trying similar cases in litigation. He was old school. He knew the difference between right and wrong, and he ended up being my greatest advocate. He brow-beat the fuck out of these attorneys, who knew the company they represented was horribly at fault. Their defense once we were face to face was so full of holes, you could tell that they personally didn't agree with what the company had done, but they had to defend it nonetheless. This Arbitrator was totally on my side, berating them for what they had put me through. At the end of the day, he had to follow the law set forth by the agreement you had to sign as a rideshare driver on their platform – waiving any right to compensatory claims against them as your employer. This is why rideshare drivers should unionize. They are getting fucked more than they know. The company receives an absurd cut out of the ride fare, forcing drivers to drive that much more to end up making that difference back. Shit for some of us they were taking almost a third of the fare. On top of that they had impunity to withhold any or all wages earned at their discretion. In my case it took me almost 365 calendar days to receive a check, and it was only for the amount of the fare. Was I happy, fuck yeah I was. They may have thought that they could delay and delay, to dissuade me from continuing with my suit. But this was the difference between right and wrong. If I couldn't stand up for myself in this circumstance, what example would I be showing my children? I won, they lost. They tried to screw over the little guy, I wasn't going to let that happen.

I would have loved swearing off rideshare driving for good, but in many cases I still needed the money. That's when I decided to solely drive for the nicer of the two rideshare behemoths. I would do so really until the pandemic hit. That's when I decided it wasn't as lucrative as it had once been, and surely not for the chance of getting sick. The sad part is that there are so many others that didn't have that option. I had to make serious cutbacks in my life in order to make it work without that additional source of income.

I was homeless for a few months as a result. However despite the stress of being homeless, I knew I couldn't go any longer working 24 hours around the clock, shit just wasn't healthy. What is the definition of insanity? It's doing the same thing over and over again, and expecting a different result. The result for me would be putting myself into an early grave. It wasn't sustainable, and I would end up having back problems as a result of the constant sitting, problems that still persist to this day. I would end up getting myself out of that level of poverty, but it would continue to be a result of hard work and further sacrifice.

CHAPTER VII.
WHERE DO WE GO FROM HERE?

Being homeless gave me incredible perspective. I had heard the saying at AA meetings all the time, "I've been everywhere from Park Avenue to the park bench." That saying certainly applied to my circumstances. The fact that I had built myself up to a certain level, only to collapse like a house of cards, gave me the drive and persistence to pursue the lifestyle I had so much enjoyed in years past. That was my saving grace. Knowing where I came from, where I had been thereafter, and the need to return back to some semblance of the good old times in years past. This was piece by piece my mantra to move forward.

My dad always used a term that I love, symbolism for taking on in some cases insurmountable tasks. "How do you eat and elephant Justin?" he'd ask. "One bite at a time" he'd answer back. It would end up taking me years to figure out how to get myself out of the rut that I was in. Today, times are not as great as I'd like them to be, but they're certainly leading in the right direction. I realize that these changes cannot come about overnight as my impatience would like them to.

I would realize that I'd never become the person I was, too much had happened, those mental scars just don't go away. I know that what I had gone through had drawn a lot of positives in creating mental fortitude.

In years past I would have to turn people down when invited to go do things. Things I really wanted to do I would deny myself of because I was too embarrassed at the situation I was in. For those inviting me, I couldn't open up to the real reasons why I would object. I had a hard time admitting I was broke mentally and financially, perpetually sad I had a hard time looking at people in the eye. I had lost a lot of my confidence. When asked by my coworkers at my fulltime job as to what 'fun plans do I have for the weekend?' I could never truthfully respond. I had a hard time admitting that my 'fun plans for the weekend' entailed driving for hours and hours on end just to break even. I've had a lot of hands in my cookie jar for years, so it was difficult for me to admit I was having money troubles, even when they were making as much as I did. I didn't have any discretionary spending money, everything I had earned went straight to my kids or ensuring I didn't have to sleep in my car at the Wal-Mart parking lot.

These actions have created a social recluse. I never was that way. I loved being around people, making people laugh, and lending a helping hand any way I could. When I had money, I shared it. I used to love hosting parties and barbecues. I loved cooking for people. I'd go to the store and buy a bunch of different kinds of meat, and work hours prior to, getting everything ready to show my friends a good time. When I was broke, that all went by the wayside, and it certainly would have an impact on my sociability thereafter.

I'm trying to get better, but it's a struggle, and certainly not the linear recovery I would have liked to have had. Yet I've learned so much about myself, about other people and their struggles, and how to react to society as a result. When I was homeless I saw it all firsthand. My homelessness was basically a choice, but a tough choice nonetheless. I had bills that I would continue to pay, that in certain circumstances impeded my way of feeding myself. But in paying those bills it gave me a sense of pride that I was doing the right thing. I always ensured my kids were taken care of, even if I could only see them a fraction of the time. In many cases they are the reason why I am still here alive and kicking ass today. Did taking my life ever cross my mind, absolutely. How could it not in the state of mind I was in at the time?! But it was the love for my family and the responsibility to my children to be every bit of a father I could be to them, that would always get me out of that funk. I realize that not everyone with mental illness is in that same position.

I chose to be homeless for the simple fact that I had more money going out than I had coming in. I couldn't move in with family as they all lived too far from my full-time job at the time. It was a function of saving every bit I could to be able to afford a deposit on a place to live – a place for my children and I to be together. The weekends I would have them I made every effort to give them the impression that I was doing just fine, but it still would prove to be challenging. They'd ask, "Daddy, why do we have to stay at the Motel 6 on the weekends we are with you?" Thinking to myself that that was the only place I could afford. No way could I tell them that the other 11 days between seeing them I was sleeping in my car at the Wal-Mart Parking lot in Dixon. My gym membership to 24 hour fitness, a membership I used to use all the time working out and staying in shape, now was for the sole purpose of taking a hot shower. I would have a storage unit where every few days I'd pick up clean clothes to wear, and every few days thereafter dropping off clean clothes I was able to wash at the laundry mat. No one at my office knew I was homeless, I made damn sure I didn't. How can the bank's Financial Advisor be homeless, wouldn't that make him a shitty financial advisor since he's broke and cannot afford a roof over his head? I loved what I did. I was great at assessing people's risk tolerance and financial needs when planning for retirement. Just because I didn't have any money didn't mean I wasn't good at managing money for others.

Over time I was able to get into a 1 bedroom shoebox of an apartment. We would have 3 beds in the bedroom, living on top of each other my kids and I. This was something I was incredibly proud of though. Having my own roof over my head and not having to worry about being woken up in the middle of the night and the stress therein was imperative to my recovery. I'm slowly on track to get myself out of debt, and my hopes are for one day soon to be able to rent a home where my kids can have their own bedrooms. It's stressful seeing them grow up so quickly, that sometimes it feels like I'm running out of time to do so.

I'm trying to be more social. I talk more with my peers at work, my neighbors, and certainly parents, brother, and sister. I have a beautiful niece that is another light of my life, and I thoroughly enjoy the time I spend with her and my kids together.

My long-term goals are to pursue additional education to put me in a better position to earn within the industry I love working. My hope is that with the additional income, I could provide my children with the life that I so much want to give them. They deserve better. It was hard coming to this realization. Having this cloud above my head for so long, though the changes are slight and slow in movement, I am headed in the right direction. For me writing this book is a huge part of my recovery. I know my story has merit. Not only does it provide me a means to learn from my own mistakes and accomplishments, but it is my hope that those reading this can find value in their recovery as well. For the longest time I was embarrassed to admit I had mental illness. For me it was my scarlet letter, the brand on my forehead, alerting everyone to everything that was wrong with me.

The title of my book *Hello my name is Bipolar,* is my journey, it is who I am. I had got the idea from watching the movie The Joker with Joaquin Phoenix. He would have these bouts of laughing when put in nervous situations. He had a business card that he'd share with those around him to show that he had this mental illness that prevented him from stopping. This scene had really resonated with me as I wish at times I had a card with my affliction written on it as a means to communicate the mental illness that I was experiencing. Now creating business cards has a lot of symbolism, but in the real world I could only view it as a means to deflect. I wrote a book to accept my struggles. It's through facing them head on that I have had the ability to recover.

Hope is never lost, it just takes some of us a change in our lives to find it again. It took me an incredible journey to realize that mental illness was not something I would ever be able to escape. However it is something I had to embrace, understand, and only then could I truly recover on my terms. I hope my story has helped you in some way, in any way – that's why I wrote it.

Hello my name is Justin, and I am Bipolar. Thank you for reading.

9 798395 849182